M000045029

I Am a Teamster

A Short, Fiery Story of Regina V. Polk, Her Hats, Her Pets, Sweet
Love, and the Modern-Day Labor Movement

by

Terry Spencer Hesser

First Edition

Lake Claremont Press
Chicago
www.lakeclaremont.com

I Am a Teamster: A Short, Fiery Story of Regina V. Polk, Her Hats, Her Pets, Sweet Love, and the Modern-Day Labor Movement

Terry Spencer Hesser

Published May 2008 by:

LAKE CLAREMONT PRESS
www.lakeclaremont.com

P.O. Box 711
Chicago, IL 60690-0711
lcp@lakeclaremont.com

Publisher's Cataloging-In-Publication Data
(Prepared by The Donohue Group, Inc.)

Hesser, Terry Spencer.
   I am a Teamster : a short, fiery story of Regina V. Polk, her hats, her pets, sweet love, and the modern-day labor movement / by Terry Spencer Hesser. — 1st ed.

   p. : ill. ; cm.

   Includes index.
   ISBN: 978-1-893121-35-5

1. Polk, Regina V. 2. International Brotherhood of Teamsters, Chauffeurs, Warehousemen, and Helpers of America—Biography. 3. Women labor leaders—Illinois—Biography. 4. Labor unions—Illinois—20th century—History. 5. White collar workers—Labor unions—Illinois—20th century—History. 6. Women—Employment—United States—History. I. Title.

HD8073.P655 H47 2008
331.88/11/38050973/092
2008925798

11 10 09 08   10 9 8 7 6 5 4 3 2 1

To Kira, my inspiration, my aspiration, my role model, my companion, my teacher, my daughter. For all the joy you have given me. And for believing in me when I lost faith in myself. I'm honored to call you mine.

Eulogy

Gina Polk was a fighter. She struggled for the rights of unorganized workers to join a union. She championed the rights of union members to get the best contract possible, and then to make sure they received the full benefits of their contracts.

In a speech Gina gave on May 9, 1981, she said, "We must constantly defend and protect the things we've won—and not just at contract time. We must always guard against the erosion of our contracts, for no matter how many shortcomings you may think of your contract having, it is the most precious thing that exists for us in the workplace." In life and as we remember her, Gina was a realist who saw the necessity of big labor as a counterbalance for big business. She lived as she believed and felt that it was more important to actually help one person than talk about saving the world.

Her entire career was with the International Brotherhood of Teamsters Local 743. She was proud to be a Teamster, proud of the union's accomplishments, and she constantly worked to make it better.

I feel that she died in the line of duty. She was on the way to a meeting that would give dislocated workers better access to job training. She had, of late, been to many such meetings but was always willing to go the entire mile if it would help her members.

This eulogy would not be complete without mentioning Gina's devotion to animals, cooking, hats, shoes, trips to Elizabeth Arden, her family, and her friends. Above all, she was a devoted and wonderful wife. But most of all, she would want each of us to remember her as she was—a woman who cared.

—Tom Heagy

Teamster's Devotion Costs Her Life, But Her Spirit Lives On

Teamster officers do their job every day, serving their brothers and sisters in the union movement with determination and dedication. For one such field soldier, Teamsters Local 743 Business Representative Regina V. Polk, the battle ended all too swiftly when, while on a mission to help people, she was killed with 10 others on October 11, 1983, in the crash of an Air Illinois plane.

Polk's death ended the life of a brilliant, beautiful and courageous young woman, whose first experience with solidarity had come while she was a student in the graduate school of business at the University of Chicago in 1974, working part-time as a waitress. Experiencing injustice first-hand when she was fired for leading a protest against working conditions, Polk sought help from Teamsters Local 743, and after winning her grievance against the restaurant, gravitated to the union movement after finishing academic training in industrial relations at the University of Chicago. A flame had been lit that would live on through her life.

This courageous Teamster's commitment and contributions were recently immortalized through the establishment of a scholarship in Polk's honor, one that will focus on training "highly committed individuals to pursue careers in the labor movement."

Polk had a fierce dedication to the union movement, as evidenced by remarks made to a Local 743 Stewards' Conference in 1981.

"You took the job as steward because you believe in the dig-

Regina V. Polk

nity of work and those who earn their living by it. You believe that every person who works should bow their heads to no one. You believe in the right of workers to make decisions about those things that affect their lives. You believe that every person is entitled to the best price for their toil. You believe in the dignity and respect and rights that come only from a written contract. And most of all, you believe it is your duty to protect all those things. It is your primary job to be constantly on guard for those who would take from us the only thing that gives our work meaning and dignity—the right to speak freely. The right to challenge and the right to participate.

"When there is no union, there are no rights. There is only silence."

Those rousing words proved that Regina V. Polk had learned well the meaning of trade unionism . . . not from books, though she had read widely . . . not in university classrooms, though she was an eager student . . . but in the crucible of the around-the-clock organizing campaigns . . . the house calls . . . the hundreds of meetings . . . not from her point of view,

but from men and women seeking a lift through organization.

When a major firm with which Local 743 had a long and productive collective bargaining relationship went out of business, Regina Polk was given responsibility for establishing programs to retrain workers who lost their jobs because of layoffs and plant closings. She sought out the experts in the field and the sources of public and private funds for this purpose.

Just days before her death in the air crash on the way to Carbondale, Illinois for a meeting of the Illinois Jobs Coordination Council, she witnessed the graduation of the first class of displaced workers, designed to upgrade their reading and writing skills. Some later achieved their goals: jobs for which they were qualified, because Regina Polk pointed the way.

Polk's husband, Thomas C. Heagy decided on the scholarship fund as a fitting memorial to the Teamster because, as he said, "She was convinced that the future of the labor movement depended upon developing creative leadership committed to organizing white collar workers, increasing the number of women in union leadership roles and retraining workers for new job opportunities."

Contributions to the Regina V. Polk Scholarship Fund for Labor Leadership have been made by both Local 743 and the International Union, both of which believe it to be a sound investment in the kind of vigorous trade union movement Regina would have served so well if she had been granted more years in which to use her unusual talent.

Not forgotten.

Courtesy of *The International Teamster*, May 1984.

Table of Contents

Regina V. Polk, exploring the world.

♥ *Prologue*

█████████████████████████████████

I only met Regina Polk once. Briefly. She came to the bank where I worked to visit her husband and stopped to say hello to my boss at the time, Sarah Brown. Regina was dressed very dramatically, her wide smile competing with a gigantic hat. Both, however, were simultaneously eclipsed by an enthusiastic assertion of self-confidence. She was only a few years older than I was at the time (she about 32, I about 28) but seemed light-years ahead of me in terms of something that I can only recall as a certainty in herself, in her mission, in her ability. *(That's a Teamster?* I thought. *The beauty? The cape? The high heels? The perfect make-up? Where's the beer belly and the donut? The scowl and the crowbar?)*

In my research, Regina has been described to me over and over again as a beautiful woman of some mystery, tremendous passion, and great self-confidence. She clearly made a lasting and profound impression on every single person she met—whether they liked her, loved her, or not.

One of the photographs I have of Regina Polk has haunted and helped me a great deal through the process of trying to understand who she was, decode the message of her life, and figure out why she was able to do what she did with such a powerful loyalty to her convictions. In the photo, she is about 28 years old. Her copper hair is covered with a scarf tied in the Bolshevik style that Americans coveted in the early 1970s. Behind her enormous mock aviator glasses, her green eyes look confidently and somehow kindly into the camera. *You immediately trust her.* Her nose is nearly Roman. *You also envy her beauty.* Her lips are pressed together into a small smile that reveals determination, confidence, and perhaps something like patience. *You admire her.* Between her eyebrows is a small birthmark in the shape of half a heart. *An accident of pigment or a sign?* She is beautiful and formidable at once—someone about to make her mark on the world.

This is her story—the legacy of a young woman who joined the labor movement at a precarious time in American history and fought hard to bridge the vast disparities between the power of owners and the dignity of workers. As a Teamster organizer and business agent in the late '70s and early '80s, Regina was one of the first females on the professional staff of the International Brotherhood of Teamsters and among the first to organize the neglected yet beleaguered so-called white-collar workers—clerks, typists, secretaries, and librarians—who faced the same problems as their brethren working in the factories or driving the trucks but with more complicated psychological allegiances to their employers. Along the way, she (like her idol Jimmy Hoffa) would find herself surrounded by allies (as well as enemies) of dubious character from without and within the union. Allies who became her teachers and mentors, and enemies with whom she battled boldly as she worked to further her goals of empowering the American worker— mostly women—in an environment characterized by male dominance. Public disgrace, violence, corruption, and ties to organized crime were discrediting Labor from within, and greed, deregulation, Reaganomics, and union busting were dismantling it from without.

But Regina Polk cared about individual rights. She particularly cared about women struggling silently in the workplace and fought to give them a voice as well as better pay, better benefits, and a modicum of respect through membership in the most powerful union in America. In return, the people she organized believed in her. They trusted her and, hence, her local, despite the national scandals and powerful opposition that plagued the Teamsters Union—so much so that many clung to the hope that Regina Polk would successfully keep the dream of solidarity alive and put an end to the calculated indignities that existed (and still do exist) in the workplace. She might have done just that. *Had she lived beyond the age of 33.*

 *Arizona*

*O*n February 14, 1950, Regina V. Polk was born to cotton and alfalfa farmers in Casa Grande, Arizona. Older sister Eileen's first two-year-old memory is of going to the hospital to select one baby from all of the babies that they had to offer.

"I selected the one with a small birthmark between her eyebrows in the shape of a valentine heart on its side," Eileen recalls. Spiritualists would say she was marked with goodness. Later, nearly everyone would say it.

At the time of Regina's birth, her parents, Helen and Henry Polk, were 44 and 47 years old—old enough to be her grandparents, especially in the rural Southwest. Their life as farmers was difficult and often impoverished. It was a life that called to Henry and one that Helen adapted to in middle age.

Helen had been raised in a cultured middle Pennsylvania home to parents of German descent. The youngest of five, she was intelligent, accomplished, independent, and well acquainted with the Protestant work ethic that espouses positive results through hard work and perfectionism.

Yet, no matter how hard she tried, Helen could not tame her physical body. She was a chubby child who became a "big" adult and was continually chided for not being small enough to suit the proportions allotted to women in the world as she knew it.

After she graduated from nursing school and worked for several years as a school and camp nurse, Helen's desire for a bigger life manifested itself in the romantic idea of going west. It was a rebellious move. At the time, American women sought security and stability over adventure and independence. But Helen, then in her 30s, got into her car and drove across the country by herself, leaving everything behind but the treasured family china and silverware given to her by her mother. She must have been scared and probably exhilarated as well. It's impossible to know what she expected out of her adventure, but what she found, initially, was a job as a civilian nurse with the Navy in San Pedro, California.

Henry was from a poor Texas farm family. One of six children, he attended school through the 8th grade and eventually left home as a teenager to join the Navy. After serving aboard the USS *New Mexico* for a tour of duty, he returned to Texas for a short time. Then, like Helen, Henry answered some inner siren's call and migrated west to embrace his own fate. After working a farm in Arizona, he moved to San Pedro, California, as well and found work in the Navy shipyards as a civilian carpenter.

It was in San Pedro that he met his wives: Alice and Helen. With Alice, he enjoyed a brief happy first marriage. But Alice died from breast cancer in August of 1944. The still-mourning Henry then married Alice's friend Helen the following year.

"I think Dad was 'rebounding' when he and Mom got together," recalls Regina's older sister, Eileen. "Not to say they didn't care for each other, but I think there was always a bit of regret on my dad's part for having remarried so soon." For Helen's part, Eileen speculates that, "in some way my mom figured she might not find another man who would accept her as she was—a big woman."

When the war was over, Henry and his new wife, still getting to know each other, moved to Arizona, where Helen quickly learned what it meant to be an itinerant farmer's wife.

Living at the whim of nature as well as luck, they spent their first years together renting or leasing a series of farms around the greater Phoenix Valley and Prescott area, where Henry taught Helen the back-breaking labor of farming.

The life was hard for two people nearing 50. Their differences in ability and temperament were vast. Helen was educated, independent minded, and burdened by her heavy-set frame. Henry was practical, traditional, and reed thin. Helen liked opera and classical music. Henry liked old-time country and gospel. Helen liked painting and sculpture. Henry liked landscapes and carvings created by nature. That duality would eventually find itself represented in the personalities of their two daughters.

"Their record collections were amazingly dissimilar!" recalls Eileen. "I remember the 45 RPM records so well. Mom's included Brahms and Beethoven. Daddy's had Eddie Arnold, Hank Snow, and the Chuck Wagon Gang."

Though the circumstances were probably not what she had imagined when leaving Pennsylvania to expand her horizons, Helen graciously (and sometimes, no doubt, not so graciously) accepted her fate as wife of a poor, traditional-thinking farmer. The family consistently lived miles from the nearest town. There were never any cultural activities. And even if there had been, Helen would probably have been too tired to go after a long day on the farm.

On Henry's part, although his second wife rose with him before the sun and worked steadily until late at night, he could sense her chafing at the narrow boundaries and ideas of the only life he knew. "Not to say they didn't grow to love and respect each other," says Eileen, "but there was always *something* between them that made it feel theirs was not a match made in heaven."

When their first daughter, Eileen, was a baby, the Polks took a much-needed break from their farm outside of Prescott. It was early in their marriage and Helen was still learning about the harsh realities of farming and mothering. To escape for a short weekend, they packed up their car and drove to Phoenix to visit friends. While they were gone, their home caught fire. They lost everything—all their clothing and furniture as well as the last vestiges of Helen's former life: the lovely bone china, silver, and photographs documenting the life and family that she had left behind in Pennsylvania. Upon their return, they witnessed only a pile of ashes and the smell of disaster. Helen in particular was devastated.

"Later in her life," says Eileen, "Regina was always buying things for my folks. I think she always thought in the back of her mind that Mom had lost all of her lovely things and Gina ached inside for what that loss must have felt like."

While living outside of Casa Grande on a place called the Tweedy Ranch and still recovering from the devastating demise of her past as well as her present, Helen gave birth to a second daughter—a girl marked with half of a heart between her eyebrows—on Valentine's Day, 1950. "Gina was born at 3:47 A.M.," Eileen muses. "Maybe [that hour] was an indication that she was going to be someone who would cause people to lose sleep throughout the coming years?"

Eileen is right. From birth, the baby marked with love was not marked with complacency. Active, fearless, and colicky, Regina wouldn't sit still. Or go along to get along. Ever. In a photo taken around 1952 in Picacho Peak State Park, between Casa Grande and Tucson, Regina's father, wizened and lean, is kneeling next to his car, flanked by his two blonde daughters. The occasion was a rare Sunday when Henry was able to take the day off from farming to go on a family outing for a few hours. Eileen is smiling happily (obediently?) at the camera. Regina, wearing cowboy boots and a frown, has both hands folded into fists (not so obediently?). She was clearly not enjoying the inactivity of posing for a portrait and was revealing her authentic feelings of frustration at the restriction. She was, what people called, a handful.

As a result of her age, responsibilities on the farm, and physical limitations, Helen came to depend heavily on Eileen, little more than a baby herself, to help with her assertive little sister as the family moved periodically to new farms throughout Arizona.

As the Polk girls grew up, Eileen and Regina revealed themselves to be as different in taste and temperament as their parents were. Eileen physically resembled her mother and tended to put on weight. She was quiet, shy, emotionally reserved, fearful of bucking authority, and she liked to blend into a crowd without drawing attention to herself. Undemonstrative, she revealed even her love for her parents in a soft and almost unspoken way.

Regina was thin like her father but had her mother's independent streak. She was emotionally and physically demonstrative in her affection and unafraid of showing dissatisfaction. She was reckless. She wanted to be the first to do anything, and if it had already been done, she wanted to do it better. Even more free-spirited than her mother had once been and without the strict Protestant upbringing, Regina was a natural iconoclast—someone who seemed to be continually testing other people's beliefs, pushing the limits, and stretching the boundaries without concern for repercussions. But despite the disharmony that her temperament mandated, for the rest of her life, fists clenched or not, wherever Regina went, she received notice and admiration for her beauty, her boldness, and her authenticity.

"My dad loved to tell the story of how once he sent Gina and me down into the fields to set a new head of water to irrigate the field," recalls Eileen. When the "dam" the sisters built across the irrigation ditch didn't hold, Eileen ran off to find their father for help. When the pair returned to the field, they found Regina sitting in the ditch, using her body to stop the water from flowing. "He got the biggest chuckle out of that," says Eileen with some awe. "I guess way back then she had such determination to get things done, no matter *how* you do it!"

As the Polks moved from farm to farm, Regina's compassion for animals expanded into a lifelong passion. And usually she was drawn most not to just any animal but to the smallest, frailest, and most at risk. It was these that she chose to love and nurture. "She would continually gravitate toward the runt of any of the litters born or hatched," says Eileen, "and lavish them with motherly attention, often hand-feeding, cuddling, and even sleeping with her new dependents—if she could get them past our parents."

A favorite family story involves Regina latching onto a baby chick and lavishing it with attention for weeks, often sleeping with it in the barn until it became "her best buddy." Her fowl friend turned out to be male—a small rooster, which she entered in their little town's annual Christmas pet parade, after making it a little jacket to wear for the occasion.

Not that Regina's ardor for animals didn't cause problems. When she was about six years old she tried to "save" a mouse and bring it home with her, resulting in her needing a series of painful rabies shots, which did nothing to diminish her devotion or increase her sense of self-protection. A few years later came another bite and more nasty repercussions. "I can't remember what it was [that bit her]," says Eileen, "but she again had to have rabies shots. I remember my mom giving her the painful shots in her stomach every day.

"Before Regina even knew what social justice meant," Eileen recalls, "she was out there, fighting for the proverbial underdog. Whether it was with people or animals, she loved helping others. When she was in fourth grade, her teacher wrote in a report card that Regina was the most compassionate child she had ever seen."

When Regina was in grammar school, the family eventually settled in Wilcox, Arizona, where they bought 200 acres and built a house. To offset their expenses, Helen took a job nursing at the local hospital and left a little more of the farm and housework to Henry and the girls. That added burden might have been the tipping point for Eileen as the sisters' differences spilled over into full-blown physical fights over the division of labor on the farm.

"We always used to fight over who was going to do what chores," says Eileen. "Especially during the summer, we were expected to help out my dad on the farm. Usually what happened is that one of us would need to go with my dad to work out in the fields in some capacity, and the other was supposed to stay at the house and do housework. Neither of us liked housework so we were always arguing and fighting over who was going to do what. Also, we had to take turns doing the milking in the mornings before school and the evenings after school. When one of us wanted to swap duties it usually resulted in some kind of fight over whose turn it was to do what. This also spilled over to household chores like doing the dishes. My folks usually had to take matters in hand and assign us. Sometimes we both got to work with my dad and we usually got along okay then."

By the time Eileen was in high school, working on the yearbook and participating in Future Homemakers of America, Regina was developing into a somewhat moody tomboy. "I remember Gina doing a lot of pouting and closing herself off in her room, or riding away on her bike when she was younger," recalls Eileen. "I think she sometimes talked back, which could get her into trouble, especially if the tone of voice was disrespectful. But she did a lot of that with me, too. I'm sure there were many times when Gina felt in her heart and soul that I was Mom's favorite, and I'm sure to a younger person who isn't always able to understand or accept differential treatment of siblings, she had to react in the only way she knew how, and that was to lash out, both at me and at Mom."

While those eruptions remained verbal with her mother, Regina and Eileen frequently took out their frustration with each other physically. "While I have no strong recollection of what caused the fights," says Eileen, "my sense is that I must have felt jealousy toward her and I think I felt intimidated by her and her actions at times. She was often skirting on the edge of authority, and I couldn't understand that. I must have been mean to her a lot but I don't know why. It must have been my way of coping with her ability to stand out in the crowd, so to speak. While I didn't seek that kind of attention myself, I guess maybe I was envious that she was able to garner that for herself—no matter that it was negative sometimes."

Henry became Regina's ally in the Polk household. Not a passionate man himself, he was nevertheless tolerant of his youngest daughter's fiery temperament—even when her rebukes were directed at him.

"My dad was raised in an environment where it was common to call black people 'niggers,'" recalls Eileen. "Every now and then my dad would use the word—not in a directly demeaning way, but it was still a hot button for Gina. Dad might say something like, 'I hired old John the nigger to do XXX job for me,' and Gina would get very feisty and indignant, put her hands on her hips, and say, '*Daddy*! That's not a nice word to use!' And he'd kind of agree with her that the word wasn't right to use. But of course he'd slip and use it again, and then he'd hear from Gina again."

As Regina grew into a teenager, she was a constant rabble-rouser, often asking her father to intercede on her behalf with her mother, who continually tried to reel in the passions of her headstrong daughter. "She wanted to go places and do things that didn't always meet with the approval of our parents, but she never thought twice about asserting herself and letting her opinions be known," says Eileen with love and sympathy for the job of a parent.

"Regina was never subtle and often moody, temperamental, and crabby. She valued independence and autonomy in a woman (rather like Mom), even though we didn't know what that was all about in those days. We just thought Gina was a pain in the butt."

While Gina would continue to clash with her mother for the rest of her life, the two loved each other deeply, each seeing herself in the assertion of will and aching immediate wants and needs of the other. Each wanting to care for and protect the other. But while Helen in middle age had decided to repress her independence to fit into the confines of her narrow world, Regina celebrated herself at an early age, pushed back at the boundaries, and gave her own intellect, emotions, and determination full sway.

By the time she was a freshman at Willcox High, Regina could throw a ball farther than many of the boys, and she dabbled in drumming. She joined the Civil Air Patrol and got involved in a number of rescue and recovery air operations in southeastern Arizona.

When not riding in rescue planes as a spotter, the bold 14-year-old worked on the ground to help the adult crews strategize where to look for a missing or downed plane. She was awarded and acclaimed for her efforts.

"She attended a Civil Air Patrol event in Texas and came home with a huge trophy for some accomplishment—I don't recall what it was," says Eileen. "I do remember she was embarrassed by the award and played down the fact that she won it. This was always her way. She did good things, but yet did not want to be singled out for praise—and I think that is part of her makeup. She did good for good's sake—not for any recognition or thanks."

At another Civil Air Patrol event in Tucson, the 14-year-old met her first serious boyfriend, a high school senior, and set off a new series of worries for her parents. She was not only popular with boys; she liked them—and herself through their adoring eyes.

"I think my mom was always kind of afraid of Gina jumping head-first into things, including relationships. Afraid that she was going to get hurt, Mom wanted her to slow down and take things more cautiously, and Gina would have no part of it."

The long-distance relationship was put to an abrupt end halfway through Regina's freshman year of high school when Henry retired and moved the family to Paradise, California. With her first heartbreak under her belt, Regina's impetuous nature continued to blossom along with her intellect and independence.

Henry Polk at work on Tweedy Ranch, mid-1940s.

Helen and Henry Polk on vacation with the Heagys, Honolulu.

**Eileen, Henry, and Regina (with clenched fists) Polk
in the Arizona sunshine, 1954.**

Helen, Henry, and Lake Michigan's finest sushi.

Eileen, left, and Regina Polk, 1954.

Regina, Paradise California
High School, 1967.

Regina, Mills College,
California, 1972.

California

othing like the Arizona farms Regina was used to, Paradise was a scenic town nestled into the beautiful foothills of the Sierra Nevada mountains in Northern California. It was a John Birch Society town consisting of conservative, communist-fearing, free enterprise–promoting, God-invoking patriots whose mission was and is to achieve "Less Government, More Responsibility, and—With God's Help—a Better World." During the 1960s, the John Birch Society opposed the civil rights movement based on their belief that it was backed and supported by the American Communist Party. Today, the society's solution to immigration reform is simple: reduce the number of illegal immigrants. But in 1965 there were no blacks or Hispanics to worry about in the town of Paradise.

Despite Regina's sorrow over leaving her home, her friends, her school, and her long-distance boyfriend, she quickly established herself at Paradise High as someone everyone wanted to get to know.

"I'll never forget the first day she walked into our third-period English class," says her high school friend Shelley Carter. "It was winter time and she walked in with her head high and her chest out and waited for the teacher to tell her where to sit. She was gorgeous but a different kind of gorgeous. Not cheerleader gorgeous. She had strong arms and legs and a tummy. But she was confident. No nonsense. Just, *I am here. I am present.* And it wasn't as though she did it for the rest of us in the room. The room could have been empty and she would have done the same thing."

Regina's comportment and confidence extended to activities as well as opinions that were not usually embraced by girls at that time, especially in rural conservative places. She played baseball and touch football and was so accomplished as a drummer that, while still a freshman, she became the first female bass drummer in the varsity band. Regina didn't take delight in ignoring traditional gender roles—she simply never gave them a thought.

"She could twirl those drumsticks like nobody we'd ever seen," says Shelley. "And she could throw a baseball further than the boys! Regina was moving toward not being a typical female. Feminine was just feminine and she was much more than that. It was just so appealing to have a woman (a 14-year-old woman at that) who would ask, 'How come there's no volleyball after school?' It was much more like what someone would say today. But then, we never thought about doing it!"

In addition to Shelley, Regina's inner social circle included four other girls as well: Karen Guckert, Kathy Wheeler, Linda David, and Barbara Cobery. The six girls, half conservative (Karen, Kathy, and Barbara) and half liberal (Shelley, Linda, and Regina) became inseparable for the rest of high school.

"Regina laughed at jokes but didn't tell jokes," recalls Shelley. "She wasn't that kind of a storyteller but would laugh a lot. In our group, there was no defined leader. Each of us would think of things to do that were appealing to the others. It was a small town so we had to make up fun as it went—like skinny-dipping in the cold water of the Feather River. Regina needed to be around other girls who were fairly strong and knew who they were," says Shelley. "She didn't try to compete unless the other person wanted to and then she wouldn't compete solely to win. Her feeling was that competition raises the bar and everyone goes further together. She was lively rather than egotistical."

She was also progressive and self-directed. "This was the middle '60s and the women's movement hadn't really touched us yet, but Regina would talk about her very strong desire to be free," says Shelley. "Although she loved boys, she said she didn't want any strings attached to her. She was rather rebellious, even reckless. She read the Kinsey Report at 14 or 15 years old and talked about it."

Regina's innate faith in life and ability to bounce back quickly from disappointment were qualities that supported her strong will and independent spirit. Ignoring convention and tradition from childhood on, she insisted on living her own life as she saw fit.

Naturally, this caused problems with her mother, who had long since given up her own rebellious impulses. Echoing Eileen's observations, Shelley, who would become Regina's best friend and closest confidante, watched the friction between Gina and her mother escalate throughout high school. "Mrs. Polk was raised Pennsylvania German. She was conservative and believed that there were rules of how you act as a lady (rules that included not reading the Kinsey Report) and these were not rules Gina lived by. She loved her parents and they loved her but her mom couldn't put up with Gina's rebellious nature."

The summer after Regina's triumphant freshman year, Eileen rejoined the family in California and enrolled in Chico State. "I hated it and I hated California!" Eileen remembers. "But Gina was having the time of her life. She had made lots of friends. She was a tomboy, a rebel, and even then boys noticed her."

Regina's uniqueness, outspokenness, beauty, and physical abilities were even more attractive to the boys in California than they had been to the younger boys in Arizona. She quickly replaced the boyfriend she had lost with a series of new ones and cultivated a host of male friends throughout high school.

"Her relationships became a series of love tragedies," says the more careful Eileen. "She always went headfirst into these relationships, and when they crashed and burned, she was always devastated. She was a very passionate person and always put her all into everything and everyone who came her way."

Regina also proved at a young age that in personal relationships, she would not tolerate being owned or possessed. Though she was happy to share herself with another, the emotional give and take of close relationships offered as many challenges as pleasures.

"As a teenager, Regina was someone who was unforgettable to everyone whose path she crossed," says Shelley, noting the vast differences between the sisters. "Eileen always reminded me of a wise, calm, understanding, and mature spirit, whereas Gina was impulsive, opinionated, full of rebellious life, and ready to seek adventures."

One of those adventures was the relatively tame task of baking a cake at Shelley's house as a surprise for her parents. "The whole kitchen was a flurry of activity. Flour everywhere! Oh, my God! It was like, what's going on? It was the epitome of chaotic Gina-gonna-get-it-done and I was overwhelmed!"

Regina and her group of five friends were academically well matched and spent a lot of time studying together throughout high school. "In Paradise," says Shelley, "you either stayed in town or were motivated to go to school to get out."

Despite her popularity and acclaim, it isn't hard to see Regina's motivation to leave a conservative, religious, and covertly racist community of rule-conscious John Birchers. But there was another, equally compelling reason that haunted her.

"When Gina first came to town," says Shelley, "she told me she had been very, very poor growing up in Arizona and said that she would never be poor again."

🐈 College

estled amid the green, rolling foothills beneath Oakland, California, Mills College has been educating the daughters of privilege since 1871.

Today the school's Web site features a quote from a student saying, "The climate here is conducive to getting involved in issues that really matter." Regina Polk did just that. But the mental leap from the life she knew to an exclusive and expensive women's liberal arts college was one that Regina was initially unsure about.

"It was my mom who suggested to Gina that she try to go to Mills," says Eileen. "I think Mom knew Gina would do well there and I think Mom wanted her to have some prestige associated with her college education."

At first, Regina balked at the idea of an all-women's college, but once she researched it and visited the beautiful 135-acre campus accented with Mediterranean-style buildings, streams, meadows, and eucalyptus trees, she decided to give it a try but continued to downplay the honor of her acceptance.

"Gina never let on that Mills was impressive," says Shelley, who chose a college in Santa Barbara. "Her attitude was 'I'm going. I have to get out. And I'm never going to have a rural lifestyle again.'"

"I think Gina was always grateful to my mom for helping make the Mills thing happen," says Eileen. "All through the years, they often were at odds, but there was a deep and abiding love between them. Reunions were always very huggy and touchy-feely."

Because Regina knew that she wanted to help others in some capacity, she chose sociology as a major in order to learn more about the human condition. But the vast disparities between the financial and social conditions of Regina's family compared to the families of her classmates was in itself a graduate course in economic inequality.

"She was thrown into an environment crawling with rich girls from all over the world," says Eileen. "This may have been the only time Gina ever felt insecure. She never talked about it, but I remember one story where she told me that her roommate was doing something once and when Gina asked her what she was doing, the roommate stated she was clipping coupons. Gina thought it strange that a rich girl would be clipping supermarket coupons, but turns out they were some kind of coupons associated with owning bonds! Gina was so surprised."

Although Regina would come to appreciate the education and life experience that Mills had to offer, it wasn't easy at first. Living in a dormitory with wealthy girls while trying to survive on scholarships, grants, and what little help her fixed income parents could provide proved trying. "She was trying to keep up with the Mills girls and she just didn't have the means to do it," recalls Eileen. "It was then that she developed a taste for the finer things and ended up getting herself into a financial bind by overcharging on her credit."

Predictably and practically, Regina turned her attention from material matters to political ones. She met a new boyfriend who introduced her to politics and took her to antiwar demonstrations.

"Kenneth was a very dominant personality," recalls Shelley, who got an education from him as well. "When I went up to visit her in Berkeley, the three of us went to see a 1968 movie about racism in marketing on Madison Avenue. I had never in my life seen anything like it!"

Although Kenneth would eventually introduce Shelley to the man who would become her husband, his relationship with Regina didn't last long. "Their egos clashed terribly," says Shelley. "He was probably the strongest and most demanding personality that she ever dated. In part that's what she loved about him and she was sad when things came to an end, but I recall her always leaving her boyfriends with a sentiment like 'I wish it weren't but it's time to move on.'"

In her sophomore year at Mills, Regina lived with a couple of girl-friends in an apartment on campus and began a relationship with Steven, a student at Berkeley. "Gina always picked nice men to be with," says Shelley. "The majority weren't labor union people or incredibly intellectual. They were just incredibly decent human beings and they adored her."

They were also mentors and teachers. In contrast to the bucolic, pastoral, and female environment of Mills, the University of California at Berkeley was a continually unfolding discovery zone for anyone interested in social justice, civil rights, and women's issues.

"She was on campus [Berkeley] one day and a protest got out of hand," recalls Eileen. "The police were called in and just as a bystander Gina got sprayed with tear gas. She was furious at the police—and very antiestablishment during those days."

It didn't take Regina long to go from "victim/bystander" to full "warrior/participant" in the exciting extravaganza of political protest and performance art. At Berkeley, Regina embraced and enhanced her commitment to feminism and equal rights. Fearless about confronta-tions, she developed her "voice" as well as her vocabulary in the petri dish of political activism.

Though intellectually open, she also revealed a stubborn, opinionated, and inflexible aspect of her nature at that time. Her strong convictions and feelings about fairness and equality didn't always take into account human weaknesses, differences, and needs.

By her third year at Mills, Regina was living with Steven and a couple of friends off campus. It was at this time that she met one of the great loves of her life: Chelsea, a Labrador-terrier crossbreed that would become her constant companion, usually off-leash, for much of the coming decade.

But the changes in Regina's life kept coming fast and furiously. Before the end of her junior year, the newly divorced Eileen arrived from Indiana with her three-year-old-son, Michael, and moved in with Regina and the others. The previous few years had been different and much harder for Eileen than they had been for Regina.

After completing one year at Chico State, Eileen moved back to Arizona and met Bob Davich, the man who would become her first boyfriend, first husband, and father of her only child. Davich had just come back from Vietnam and was finishing his tour with the Army in Arizona. When he was discharged, he convinced Eileen to go home with him to Indiana and to marry him.

"I didn't even tell my folks I'd left Arizona," Eileen recalls. "Then when I told them I was getting married, they were beside themselves. Gina told me later that Daddy blamed Mom for my running away because she'd been too strict with me. I didn't feel that was the case. I was just young and stupid and hooked up with this handsome man who said he loved me."

Nine months and two days after Eileen's wedding day, their son Mike was born in the grimy steel town of Gary, Indiana—a landscape of rust and ruin that was as antithetical to the ones Eileen was used to as the temperaments of her rough-hewn in-laws were to those of her own family. Bob was abusive and volatile toward his wife, an attitude that was accepted and even condoned by his family. "My mom came to visit once while I was in Indiana," says Eileen. "And Gina came to visit right after Mike was born. Neither of them were impressed with Bob— or his family, for that matter."

Eileen was more than unimpressed; she was afraid. When Mike was six months old, Eileen ran away from her marriage for the first time.

"I think a lot of Bob's bad behavior was learned from his father, who knocked his mother around during their marriage and made it seem that that was the appropriate way to treat a woman," says Eileen with some sympathy. "I'm not making excuses. The way Bob treated me was wrong. But there was a good person hiding inside, albeit a confused and conflicted one."

After returning to try one more time, Eileen ran away again shortly thereafter, this time literally sneaking out while he was at work one day.

"I was in fear for my life as he'd threatened me that the only way I would ever leave him was in a pine box. I don't think he would have ever done that to me, but at the time I was scared."

After staying with her folks for a couple of months in Paradise, Eileen and Michael went to live with Gina, hoping that there would be more job opportunities for her there.

"We stayed in the big rented house with her and Steven for a few months," recalls Eileen, "then Steven moved back home to New England and the three of us moved into an apartment in Oakland."

Three-year-old Michael brought joy to both sisters. "Regina just adored Michael," says Eileen. "She loved him dearly and wanted to be very involved in his upbringing while she and I were living together."

Bob turned out to be a much better father than he had been a husband, visiting Michael in Oakland as well as hosting him in Indiana, where he proudly took his son to visit family and friends.

During that early period together, Eileen and Regina discovered each other anew. "I don't remember feeling close to her really at all until we lived together in Oakland," says Eileen. "It was then that we started forming a strong bond of love and respect for one another."

Not surprisingly, Eileen found life with Regina to be as much of a series of surprises as she had witnessed growing up with her. "Once we were in a movie theater and the people behind us were talking as the movie got under way. She turned around to these folks and said rather matter-of-factly, 'Shut the fuck up.' I remember being mortified and wanting to slink down under the seats."

Gina's self-righteousness was no surprise to her sister, but her strident, newly-acquired Berkley slang was. There were more surprises to come.

"The cops came to the door early one morning and arrested Gina," recalls Eileen, "for not paying fines for having her dog off-leash in public. I'd just arrived to California and had no idea what to do, but remembered she had a UC Berkeley friend who was a law student. I managed to contact him and he helped out in some way. I don't remember the disposition of the case, but I remember being totally shocked by my sister being taken away by the cops."

Shelley Carter laughs about the incident and Regina's reaction to it. "She told me later that on that Sunday morning, she was sitting in jail with all these hookers! Now she's as cute as she can be. Not worldly looking at all with her Nordic-blonde looks. Well, she said there was no way she could tell the hookers that she was in for a dog fine!"

Regina had not been any more scared of this arrest than she had been of the rabies shots she endured after the mouse bite. In her mind, she was once again doing what was right—in this case, allowing her dog the freedom she felt appropriate—and accepted the consequences without a thought to altering her behavior. If anything, her antiestablishment leanings increased after her arrest, and she began to feed the thrill-seeking side of her nature with new, if subversive, experiences.

Regina graduated from Mills in 1972 with a degree in sociology but continued to work at the college as a research assistant for a married professor she had been romantically involved with after Steven. When the affair ended, Regina decided that nature might offer the consolation and peace necessary to put distance between her feelings and the minor scandal brewing.

"She came home and told me she had to get out of town," recalls Eileen. "We packed up a few clothes, some food, her two dogs—Chelsea and Morgan, a mutt she adopted along the way—and the three of us piled into the old Chevy my folks had let us have for transportation and headed to Yosemite National Park. This was during the winter or early spring because there was lots of snow all over Yosemite Valley. We camped out for about three nights—and that meant we slept in the car at night as we had no tent or anything and it was so cold. Gina and the two dogs slept in the front seat and Mike and I slept in the back. People must have thought we were homeless! It was a miserable trip, but Gina needed this, so we went along with her."

Some months later, Gina decided that she needed a more serious change of scenery. She packed her beloved dogs and whatever else she could fit into her Volkswagen and drove to Albuquerque, New Mexico, where her old high school pal Shelley Carter was living at the time.

Brief Transitions

$\mathcal{F}$or about a year, Regina, Chelsea, and Morgan lived in the basement of a record store owned by Shelley and her husband, Paul. Regina got a job as a waitress at the Italian restaurant where Shelley worked, and Charles, a boyfriend who joined them later after following Regina from California, found a job working at Motorola.

"Gina made tons more tips than I did because she was just so out there!" recalls Shelley. "Some people have a separation of boundaries. Regina never measured boundaries. She was like, 'I'm here to serve you,' and she was right there with them. Lively. Engaged. Whereas I defined my job as, 'Serve them and leave them alone,' it was a completely different (and far less lucrative) approach."

On a lark, the two women decided to drive to Mexico for a little vacation. "We had a great time except for one huge argument about human rights and banking," says Shelley. "I thought that banking was part of the problem in the world and in the U.S. and said that if bankers worked on lending practices they could make a difference. Gina didn't think that the banks and bankers were solely to blame. So there we were in her old Volkswagen in Mexico having this heated argument about bankers!"

After nearly a year, Regina returned to California to find her sister happy, employed, and in a new relationship. With Regina in Albuquerque, Eileen had taken a job in the credit department of a large department store. She also met Stan, the man who would become her second husband and life partner.

"When Stan first met Gina, he thought that she was an intellectual snob," recalls Eileen. "I asked him to elaborate. He just said she had an air about her that made him think she thought she was very smart, and that she knew she was smart. He never really had a chance to know her very well."

Whatever people's impressions of Regina or her missteps, she displayed an air of confidence. High-spirited, enthusiastic, and exuberant, she wasn't content to re-experience life in a town she already knew. After having spent a year of waitressing in New Mexico, she felt that she had hibernated long enough and didn't plan to stay in California. She was restless, yearning for her next adventure and excited about the possibility of discovering something new. She enrolled in a master's program at the University of Chicago with a concentration in labor relations. In a reverse trajectory of her mother Helen's drive west three decades before, Regina, Charles, Morgan, Chelsea, and Regina's cat Stanley headed east to Chicago, often sleeping on the ground on the way.

"The boyfriend didn't last," says Eileen. "The dogs did."

Regina and Morgan, 1978.

Morgan.

Regina and Morgan, 1979.

Stanley.

Emily being fed by Regina.

Regina, Flower the cat, and Emily the rabbit.

🕸 *The Red Star Inn*

---

*D*espite its iconic logo, the Red Star Inn on Chicago's North Side had nothing whatsoever to do with workers' rights. At least until Regina got there it didn't.

To support herself while she was in graduate school, Regina secured a job as a hostess at the steak and martini mainstay just off of the Kennedy Expressway.

At 5' 7" with thick strawberry blonde hair, fine even features, and a friendly smile, Regina was a knockout by just about anyone's standards. From her podium at the hostess desk, she probably didn't have it too bad.

"Hello. . ." *"How many are in your party?"* and *"Do you have a reservation?"* would hardly have been taxing for her. But Regina immediately noticed that her coworkers were not treated as well as she was. The dishwashers, busboys, waitresses, and kitchen help were all overworked, underpaid, and verbally demeaned on a daily basis. Characteristically, Regina turned her compassion into action.

After repeatedly calling the Hotel and Restaurant Employees Union to ask for help, and repeatedly being turned down, someone finally gave Regina the phone number of Bob Simpson, Organizing Director for Teamsters Local 743.

Simpson was an imposing African-American man who was reportedly and affectionately called "Super Nigger" by none other than Jesse Jackson. Jackson spent considerable time at Local 743 to show his support for the working class, as well as to garner backing for his Operation PUSH, and was very friendly with Simpson at the time.

Even today, in retirement, Simpson's placid expression and patience with his baby grandson's requests contrast neatly with his powerful body and no-nonsense disposition. He exudes dominance. Even when handling toys.

Regina was not intimidated. She was looking for strength, power, and vigor to fight against institutionalized injustice, and she found all of those qualities in Simpson.

"My first impression of Regina," Simpson says in a characteristically quiet voice, "she came across to me as a hippie. The way she dressed and looked. She was for all kinds of rights. Worker rights. Civil rights. Women's lib."

Simpson's enthusiasm for organizing the Red Star Inn was somewhat low, and he told her so. It takes a lot of time to organize and that time costs money. He wasn't sure of winning and wasn't sure that, if they did win, it would be worth it financially. "But," as he recalls, "she kept bugging me."

In phone call after phone call Regina overcame Simpson's objections and wore down his resistance. She explained why the people at the Red Star Inn needed a union and gave example after example of how poorly the workers were treated until, finally, he gave in. "It was hard to change Regina's mind," says Bob Simpson in a typical understatement. "Once she got it into her mind and believed something or somebody, you weren't going to change it. I told her I would try to help her."

Simpson explained to Regina how the system works:

The union needs 30 percent of the employees to sign cards showing interest in the union to be eligible for consideration. Of course, this is anything but simple because employees—mostly unskilled and poor—are putting their jobs on the line should the company discover what's going on and fire them.

Because the union has to have 51 percent of the employees vote yes to win an election, organizers try to get as many employees as possible to show immediate interest to stack the deck in their favor.

Once the union has cards signed by at least 30 percent of the employees, it files a petition with the National Labor Relations Board and a date is established for an election. If 51 percent of the total employees vote in favor of a union, the business agent meets with the employees to ask them what they need. He (and eventually she) then writes the contract that will spell out exactly what the employees are asking for, and negotiations with the employer begin (hopefully). It's a long process and fraught with peril for workers as well as organizers. Employers are frequently surprised by the demand for a union. Then enraged. And finally, vindictive.

Bob gave Regina the cards and told her she needed to get them signed as quickly and as quietly as possible and wished her luck. "I told her that, by the time management finds out about us, I should be walking into their office and demanding an election."

Regina probably knew at the time that Bob never expected to see her or those signed cards ever again. But she couldn't have guessed the circumstances of their next meeting.

With a typical lack of regard for her own security, Regina whispered to her coworkers at the restaurant, met them off-site, and went to their homes. Hand-feeding them ideas and lavishing them with motherly attention, Regina was nurturing those that were the smallest, frailest, and most at risk—*people* this time—all the while hoping that she could get them safely past the parental figure, the employers.

The Red Star Inn turned out to be Teamster kindergarten for Regina Polk, and she excelled at persuading the fearful employees that they could change their circumstances. But before the union was ready to file a petition for recognition, the owner of the Red Star Inn discovered what was going on and fired for audacity the woman he hired to be acquiescent.

Upon Regina's firing, Simpson immediately arranged for Teamsters Local 743 attorney Joel D'Alba to file an unfair labor practice petition with the National Labor Relations Board. Impressed by Regina's commitment and abilities, Simpson then hired the then-unemployed but persistent young woman to do some organizing for Local 743 on a part-time basis.

Her first assignments were basic duties, such as writing leaflets and passing them out in front of factories, making phone calls to prospective members, and working picket lines. She immediately proved herself to be a great writer and tireless worker. Most importantly, the workers instantly responded to her.

"She was the kind of person that would get your attention immediately," recalls Simpson. "She had a very nice friendly smile. To know her was to love her and people naturally took a liking to her. She was such a bright outgoing person."

Under Bob Simpson's initial tutelage and support, Regina moved on to Teamsters 102. "She was very bright, very aggressive, and sincere," says Simpson. "Strictly a worker's type person. The worker was always right. She was a real trade unionist."

Not surprisingly, Regina's former employer at the Red Star Inn didn't want her back. After a review of Regina's case with the Labor Relations Board, the owners agreed to make a cash settlement in exchange for Regina not coming back to work. They had hired her as eye candy and paid a sweet amount to be rid of the entire circumstance.

For Regina's part, after a life of education and adventure, she had found her calling and wanted nothing more than to give the "union idea" her all. "She was pleased," remembers Simpson, noting that Regina didn't have any desire to go back to the restaurant.

She was also in demand. Simpson had bigger plans for the ambitious, educated young woman with the infectious smile. But first she had to interview with Local 743 president Don Peters.

"Fix yourself up," Simpson told Regina. "Wear a dress."

"I don't have a dress," was her puzzled response.

"Get one."

Stage Left

*B*y the time Regina Polk (wearing the new dress mandated by Simpson) walked into Don Peters's office for her interview in 1975, Peters had been the founder and reigning czar of Local 743 for 25 years. He was an imposing, commanding, well-connected power-house and important official in Teamster operations, nationally as well as locally. A German Lutheran from Sioux City, Iowa, Peters was a classmate of both Dear Abby and her sister Ann Landers (Essie and Eppie Lederer). When he returned from the Korean War in 1949, there was a strike at a catalog warehouse called Butler Brothers, where Peters had worked before the Army. He felt that the workers, mostly white working class, were being abused and mistreated. Through Peters's efforts, those workers became the original members of Local 743. By concentrating his efforts on similar warehouses during the 1940s and '50s, Peters managed to turn the then-obscure, 350-member local into the largest Teamsters local in the country, with more than 35,000 members during its heyday. Unlike other union officials, who typically spewed tough vitriol, Peters was a cool, polished, well-spoken maverick, pragmatist, and visionary, renowned for his intelligence, photographic memory, and ability to assess future situations and strategize responses to various possible outcomes instantly. His local was the only one that attended marches for civil rights in the South. At a time when the white working class stayed as far away from any affiliation with the black working class as possible (and America's racial boundaries made that easily possible), he convinced his members that they would all be stronger, better paid, and more respected if workers of any color and both genders supported each other. He convinced his members to risk their very lives on that premise. He also supported women's rights and had progressively begun to hire women organizers to appeal to the women they were trying to organize at a time when it was still unheard of. He courted friends in the government. He cultivated friends in the underworld. And while there has always been an affinity between the Teamsters and the mob, in Chicago it was the Irish as much as the Italians who ruled. In the web of symbiotic dependencies established to do business Chicago-style, Peters was a brilliant networker, Daley-style machinist, and great believer in the end justifying the means. He was a man known for doing whatever was necessary to attract and retain Teamster membership—not a bad fit for a woman who had once used her body as an improvised human dam to solve an irrigation problem.

By 1975, however, the times were changing again for unions. Plants were closing throughout Chicagoland and moving to Mississippi, taking the semi- to low-skilled blue- and white-collar jobs with them. And the Teamsters Union in particular was in desperate need of securing new dues-paying members. The market they had identified was the ubiquitous and growing population of white-collar, somewhat educated (mostly female) workers—a population that would, in the decade between 1970 and 1980, increase by 12.5 million to 50.5 million workers, while blue-collar laborers grew by only 2.7 million to 30.5 million workers. To organize white-collar women, the Teamsters needed a different kind of organizer to lead them out of the mire of scandal and suspicion that surrounded them on a national level.

But despite the growth potential, most unions had been avoiding female white-collar workers because they didn't have the ability to dispel the (accurate) image of themselves as aggressively male dominated. To join "the brotherhood," women would have to replace a mental picture of sticks and clubs, picket lines, beer bellies, and T-shirts with one that included a reflection of them. Their lives. Their children. Their struggles.

The problem was that the image people had of unions was an accurate one. Unions *were* exclusively and aggressively male dominated. The few women they had working for them were "girls" (no matter what their age) and usually of limited education, intelligence, and ambition—taking direction from their male bosses. Chauvinism by design. In defense of the powerbrokers, nobody gives up power willingly.

How much Regina knew about Peters or the character of Local 743 on the day of her interview is unknown. We do know that Regina believed in the union ideals with all her heart. We know that Jimmy Hoffa, whom she never met, was her personal hero. We know that she believed the Teamsters Union was the best of all possible unions because it was the strongest. We know that she believed strength was critical in dealing with the power that corporations held over people. And finally, we know that while sitting in front of Peters in a new dress-to-impress, she wanted with all of her heart and soul to be a part of the union cause in order to help the helpless.

For his part, Peters already had a sense of who Regina was. He had her impressive résumé and a recommendation from Bob Simpson. Furthermore, he had seen Regina leafletting workers at the Sears Roebuck catalog house, where the passion of her performance and the response of the workers caught his interest. He knew that when there were problems on a picket line, people would fall into two categories: the ones who disappear and the stand-up guys like Simpson. Peters had every reason to believe that Regina would be in Simpson's category.

So in the end, it wasn't the dress, her beauty, or her bearing that impressed Peters. "It was her strong interest in organizing the unorganized and her fervent belief in the union cause," Peters recalled later. "She had intelligence, passion, commitment, empathy, and a fierce desire to right the wrongs she came across."

She also had a college degree and was a woman—the combination of which made her a first at Local 743. And Peters knew exactly how to use Regina's attributes to appeal to the coveted white-collar female worker.

In that first meeting, Peters told Regina about a campaign already in progress to unionize 1,800 white-collar workers at Blue Cross/Blue Shield. Working with Muriel Carroll, the lead organizer and only female business agent at Local 743, Regina would be working to organize white-collar workers of various races who were mostly women and somewhat educated. White-collar workers who traditionally felt closer to management than to hourly production workers. White-collar women who were often more loyal to their bosses than concerned with themselves.

Gina's passion to improve women's rights, workers' rights, civil rights, and human rights had found an outlet through union solidarity. She was up for the challenge. Peters gave his nod, and Regina traded her plans for a master's degree at the University of Chicago for a full-time job as a Teamster organizer. She was thrilled.

"The union did what they do when they find a progressive worker," says D'Alba, the tall, slender, polished lawyer who had filed Regina's unfair labor practice petition with the National Labor Relations Board against the Red Star Inn. "They put her on the payroll. The year was 1975. The civil rights movement, like the women's movement, was quickly becoming a memory. Politically correct speech, obscuring and clouding all kinds of nasty realities, was beginning to complicate communication even further. And the sheen of compassion for solidarity of any kind had dulled. The union brass that had once embraced politicians and marched with them shoulder to shoulder in Labor Day parades had been replaced by owners of big business and everybody was afraid: of bosses, of being replaced, of losing their voices. Enter Regina Polk, stage left."

♥ Love

*J*ust before Regina quit graduate school at the University of Chicago to focus her talents full-time at Local 743, she met Tom Heagy, a cute young economics student who took a class in Labor Market Discrimination "to meet girls." Like her sister, Eileen, Tom was quiet and shy, though he was hardly retiring. An intellectually oriented banker, Tom had a life that was crowded with theories and numbers and thoughts that intimidated and excluded the common man (and woman) that Regina would dedicate her life to. When they met, Tom had already earned his MBA from the University of Chicago and completed a stint at the London School of Economics and was on leave from the First National Bank's First Scholars Program to pursue his Ph.D.

"Tom was a very important combination of economics and politics," says Ted Marmor, Tom's former professor (now at Yale) with whom he coauthored a paper on the politics of medical inflation. "He was the perfect example of what the University of Chicago undergraduate program was about in the '50s and '60s. Finding smart kids in America and letting them learn. An ideal student, he didn't genuflect but wasn't disrespectful."

Still, even when brimming with ideas and passions, Tom's delivery can be droll. He is a precise man and can be very intimidating. Ivory tower. His collar couldn't be stiffer, or whiter, if he were a priest. His hobbies were collecting contemporary and Asian art and going to the opera and the symphony. Hobbies with languages and structures as alien to the former farm-girl feminist and budding unionist as her proletariat passions were to him.

Regina was, by then, an outspoken champion of the people. Practically oriented. Brimming with solutions for those who couldn't begin to formulate the questions. Her social skills focused on action and results. Her hobbies were country music and cooking—both alien art forms in Tom's world, where musical notations expressed passion and boiling an egg was out of the realm of his experience.

The course where Regina met Tom was Labor Market Discrimination. One day in class, the professor, Robert Fogel (who later won a Nobel Prize in economics), posited the theory that discrimination against women was irrelevant because it didn't affect the family unit. Tom and Regina were the only students who rejected the theory as well as the underlying assumption that all women had husbands taking care of them—and they were both vocal in their passionate dismissal.

"Tom has his reform side, too," says Marmor. "He is an intellectual from a family of California schoolteachers. Good at math and interested in music. A man of high intelligence with disrespect for irrelevant hierarchy and tomfoolery. A man caught between the politics of business and the highfalutin University of Chicago."

According to Marmor, Tom Heagy was among the best graduate students he has ever had in his entire career. "And he met this lively and not superficially glamorous lady and was devastated. I sensed that she was a no-bullshit gal. A person that had all the externals of a Texas beauty queen and none of the personality manifestations."

Things they had in common: they both wore glasses, both were from California, both had strong ideas about humanitarianism, both loved good food, both had high ideals for mankind—and both were strongly attracted to the other.

"I was attracted to Regina before I even met her, before she spoke," says Tom. "And I stopped going to the class as soon as I got her phone number. I knew she was interested when she spelled her last name after giving me the phone number."

On their first date, the pair agreed to meet on the campus Midway. Regina brought chaperones. "She had two large dogs, and they were not tied up," recalls Tom. "I was so scared of her dogs that it almost put me off."

As it turned out, Tom was no more put off by her dogs than Regina was put off by the fact that Tom's idea of a good first date was a flute concert at the Lutheran Theological Seminary.

Afterward, Regina confided in Don Peters. "I met this nice man," she said simply. And she was right. Tom Heagy is a nice man. A quality sometimes hidden by his formidable intelligence and cool demeanor.

It was the beginning of a great love affair despite obvious and not-so-obvious divergent passions. She called him Thomas and he called her Gina. They were yin and yang, opposite qualities that can occasionally conspire to create powerful unions.

"Tom was seriously in love with Regina," recalls Amy Burack, a friend from graduate school.

In fact, he was so much in love with Gina that in 1977, despite his pet phobias, Tom allowed her four-legged entourage—the dogs, Chelsea (who would later be shipped back home to California) and Morgan, and the mixed-breed cat, Stanley—to move into his Hyde Park condo along with her. The condo happened to be across the street from his professor and friend Ted Marmor. In their early years together, as Tom was studying the mysteries of macroeconomics and Regina was learning that organizing was a 24-hour-a-day job, they lived unpretentiously. "Interior decoration was uninteresting to Regina," says Marmor. "They had some art and crappy furniture. She spent her little free time reading about the opera and symphony to be able to enjoy Tom's pleasures. I was the object of a respectful and cheerful generosity toward Tom's professor.

She babysat for my two girls happily."

Regina may in fact have preferred babysitting to socializing. According to Tom, "When Ted and I were discussing theories about the economy, Regina would frequently fall asleep on the couch. She was far more interested in practical action than theories."

In their first year of cohabitation (1975), Tom dropped out of his doctoral program at the University of Chicago and went to work for South Shore Bank. He would become chairman and CEO of the famous reform financial institution before he turned 30, and Regina's material world would blossom accordingly—a unique status for a Teamster.

"Regina had lived a very low-income life," says Tom. "After I gave up on my Ph.D. and went back to a bank and had income, she adapted well to the change in life. She loved hats, shoes, and, of course, animals."

Also, they traveled.

On a trip to Egypt with a group from the Oriental Institute at the University of Chicago, the couple visited El Armana, the site of Akhenathen's capital. The tour required a four-hour bus ride from Cairo, a one-hour jeep ride, followed by a half-hour donkey ride through the desert, a boat ride across the Nile, and another donkey ride to the ancient city.

"On one occasion," recalls Tom, "when everyone in the group was saying, 'Oh wow, this is the sacred city, this is amazing,' Gina said, 'There is nothing here.' It was an expression of her pragmatism."

On a trip to England that Tom planned, the couple stayed in the best hotel in Bath. "Gina was embarrassed to be staying at this fancy hotel," Tom recalls. "Then we went to a couple of other places and finally got to Stratford. In Stratford, the hotel we stayed in was more historic than fancy and when she discovered they didn't have room service she complained! After that, Regina never complained about hotels being too fancy again."

Yet, getting used to the luxuries that money can buy only enhanced Regina's passion to improve the lot of those less fortunate. At home again, she frequently coerced Tom into handing out leaflets at organizing campaigns, making phone calls, and walking picket lines—not exactly a milieu that matched Tom's comfort levels, but he did it for her.

Tom and Regina's close friend (and my former boss) Sarah Brown remembers an incident on a Saturday morning when she was preparing for a board meeting at South Shore Bank. "I was working on some flip charts for Tom's presentation when Tom rushed in wearing jeans," Sarah recalls. "He hurriedly flipped me some information for the chart as he rushed to change into business attire." Regina didn't have enough pickets that morning so Tom had been walking the picket line with her. "It was interesting to me," says Sarah, "this blend of a banker and a union organizer. Banks are not unionized and not pro-union in any way."

"She changed my mind about unions," Tom says. "When I first met her I was anti-union, but I came to understand their value." A typical understatement.

University of Cambridge, England.

University of Cambridge, England.

Warwick Castle, England.

Warwick Castle, England.

Hawaii.

Cruising the Mediterranean.

Egypt.   **Egypt.**

Egypt.

🐈 Local 743

For a woman like Regina, the challenge of organizing the mostly female white-collar workers at Blue Cross/Blue Shield must have paled in comparison to the challenges of working in the testosterone-driven primacy of Local 743. At the time, in addition to Peters, there were two alpha male business agents who ruled the local. Ray Hamilton was in charge of the white business agents and Bob Simpson was the unquestioned leader of the African-American business agents. There were cultural, racial, and attitudinal differences between the two men in an environment characterized by what today would be considered racist.

The common slur for blacks at the union hall was "shine"—disparaging, but not as hateful as "nigger." Early in her career, Regina approached a black agent and asked, "What's a shine?" He laughed and told her, "A black person." She then wanted to know the etymology. He pointed her to the nearest shoeshine stand. Regina was floored.

Ray Hamilton was a deeply religious, Irish-Catholic-American father of nine who viewed the labor movement as a historic struggle for the greater good of mankind. He was a no-nonsense maverick with a St. Ignatius education. Inspired by the gospel of Jesus, St. Ignatius students are taught to use God's gifts to promote social justice. Hamilton's personal gifts included a keen intellect as well as physical power and he brought them both into use for the union. A complicated man, he also had the Irish weakness for beer (lots of it), bullying and sarcasm, and the traditional Irish values of devotion and loyalty. He had a full face, bright blue eyes, an itch for living life head-on, and a passion for ball busting.

"My father could rationalize violence as ends justifying means," says his son Tom. "He was a very gentle man around the house, but if he felt you were on the opposite side, it was like the Nazis: as in, 'Hey, that Nazi is probably as nice a guy as I am' but he wouldn't have any problem shooting him either. [As a result] he had a lot of problems with the law." Problems like charges for battery that Peters arranged to get quietly dropped through the "Irish Mafia" that controlled Chicago's judiciary at the time.

Hamilton dropped out of DePaul University (much to the chagrin of his father) and started work unloading tires from a boxcar at BF Goodrich. After becoming a union steward, he befriended people in the Teamster hierarchy and was subsequently hired in 1957 by Don Peters at Local 743. His official job title was organizer, but his skill set included the potential for power—physical power, that is.

According to Hamilton's son Tom, Don Peters was not a man of violence and guarded himself from any direct involvement in the more brutal aspects of union life by saying something to his father like, "Jeez, I wish something bad would happen to that guy," and something bad *would* happen. The guy Peters referred to would be taking out his garbage in the morning and get a beating that would result in a settled contract. "My dad was more than happy to do it," says Hamilton. "He was a soldier and that was a logical extension of his job. Also, he was able to overcome fear to the point where he was in fights with people who he knew were carrying weapons. One guy was assembling a gun and my dad pulled him out of his truck, took away the gun, and beat him. It's a different world today."

This was the 1950s. The American economy had no competition worldwide and unions were at the height of their power. To capitalize on that power, the Teamsters, who had a lot of influence with truckers, did what was called organizational picketing. They put a picket line around an unorganized plant and refused to allow any trucks in or any trucks out.

Eventually, the frantic business owner who needed to move his products either agreed to allow his employees to become unionized or hired goons of his own. But the company goons, also predominantly Irish but of the happy-to-beat-somebody-up-for-a-beer mentality, were no match for Hamilton either physically or mentally.

Though he was a tough man, Hamilton's ability to intimidate (and hurt) people was exceeded by his intelligence. He was able to instantly assess a situation and act accordingly. And, in his Irish-Catholic soul, the union always came first, and he put fear into employers in the old-time Teamster way by saying, "Look, we'll put up a picket line and you'll be shut down tomorrow."

"Reverend Raymond," remembers Simpson fondly, "was one of the great Teamster organizers. Ray was the type of a person that cut through it all. If it meant going for beers with the boss, he would do it and get it over with. He understood how to get along with the company and the workers."

Hamilton's intelligence, loyalty, lack of fear, and physical prowess gave him access on several occasions to the big man himself: his (and Regina's) hero, Jimmy Hoffa. "He actually drove Hoffa around a couple of times in the mid '50s," says Tom Hamilton. "He acted as his bodyguard and he was enamored with him. He said that Hoffa was magnetic; he displayed charisma and power and had no interest at all in financial gain. Unlike many union guys, Hoffa was only interested in one thing, and that was power."

Hamilton's job of empowering workers put him in the middle of America's racial and cultural divides: the Italian mob, the Irish Labor

Police Detail, the frightened Jewish employers, the beleaguered old-guard white business agents, and the growing African-American membership. The stories Hamilton told contained elements of violence, racial conflict, stupidity, and greed—yet he always saw them, and in the Irish tradition retold them, as funny.

Most whites at the time were very covert in their racist views. But Hamilton was not covert. Anyone, of any race, including his own, was a potential source of mischief. And he didn't hide that opinion. After a youth spent fighting with Italians, the great black migration north began, and Hamilton, like many others of the Chicago Irish, began to think, "Gee, these ginzos aren't so bad." (Harmony between the Irish and Italians was achieved by bringing in an ethnic group even more offensive to the two groups.) Hamilton was in daily contact with tough inner-city blacks. While his dealings were confrontational, Hamilton was often very generous to, and respectful of, black people, enjoying their humor and appreciating their street smarts, even while taunting them.

Bob Simpson, on the other hand, was a big, black, aggressive, tough, and intimidating guy—every bit the worthy opponent and peer of his white coworker and competitor. Starting his union life helping to organize Montgomery Ward for Local 743, Simpson became a steward first and later joined the local as an organizer in 1963. A close personal friend of Jesse Jackson, he had been brought in as the union was moving from white to black working-class members. Smart and loyal, he in time was promoted to vice-president, served on the board of directors, and eventually became president of the union.

Peters needed Simpson because Simpson was the powerful black voice of the union. But he was also rumored to be afraid that Simpson might one day successfully run against him if the union's racial balance tilted further on the color spectrum.

To that end, Hamilton provided Peters with racial counterbalance. Peters counted on the fact that if Simpson ever presented a black slate, Hamilton would provide a white slate. The resulting tensions of the

Simpson-Hamilton détente created an atmosphere at Local 743 in which something (or someone) could blow at any minute—and often did. Yet, despite the competition and antagonism, there was an underlying respect between the two men that curtailed catastrophe.

In one particularly heated exchange, Hamilton was berating a black colleague about screwing up. The coworker played the race card and said, "Everyone knows you're antiblack."

Ray responded simply, "I'm not antiblack; I'm antidumb."

Given the relatively permissive atmosphere of the time and place, it must have taken some amount of restraint on Simpson's part not to throw a punch Hamilton's way on any number of occasions. Instead, the pointed antics and simmering animosity on both sides were as much of a presence in the office as the wrongs each sought to redress outside of it.

Simpson respected Hamilton from a distance and Hamilton genuinely liked his rival at Local 743. For all of his racist bluster, Hamilton also had a warm relationship with Jesse Jackson. When Jackson was running for president, he would tease Hamilton that he was going to put him on the ticket as his vice-president because he needed an Irish-Catholic running mate.

Hamilton also found Simpson to be funny and charming. He respected his abilities and his courage. Most importantly to Hamilton, Simpson never ran from trouble on the picket line. He was comfortable taking a stand and defending it. And, as Hamilton would reverently relate to his son Tom, "When Simpson hit you, you stayed hit."

That regard did not stop Hamilton from teasing Simpson whenever the urge struck. Hamilton had a wicked sense of humor and what would today be considered politically incorrect displays of his aptitude for dialects. Whenever he spent time with a particular group (blacks, Asians, Indians, Irish), he could affect their accents seamlessly and did so frequently.

When impersonating Bob Simpson, who Hamilton called Big Bob, he would affect a black accent with a very high pitch, which was funny because Simpson was so big (280 pounds or so at the time), often dripping with the biggest, baddest medallions fashionable in the '70s, and yet had a soft and small voice.

Hamilton's son Tom describes one occasion at Peters's friend Alan Dorfman's compound in Eagle River, Wisconsin, where the tensions between his father and Simpson could have easily erupted into violence. Dorfman frequently hosted Teamster meetings as well as social events at his Wisconsin compound because of his close association with Peters. As the stepson of Jimmy Hoffa's powerful friend Red Dorfman, Alan had been personally selected by Jimmy Hoffa to control one of the most infamous financial dynasties of modern times: the United Brotherhood of Teamsters Central States Pension Fund. He had been long recognized as the man to be seen when it came to pension loans and manipulative activities within the fund as well as the go-to guy for helping to arrange for battery charges to be quietly dropped against local 743 members when picket line or organizing activities got out of hand. He frequently hosted members of local 743 at his home in Wisconsin for boating, drinking, and socializing.

On one occasion Simpson, Peters, and Dorfman sat down to play cards and Hamilton (who didn't play cards) walked into town to buy some beer. At the tiny country store, Hamilton discovered a large cowbell hanging on a chain. He immediately bought it and put it on in scandalous parody of the gold chains and paraphernalia favored by hip black men (such as Bob Simpson) at the time.

From inside the compound, the men heard the bell ringing but had no idea where it was coming from until Hamilton opened the door and fixed his gaze on Simpson. Simpson stopped dealing the cards and stared at him. At the cow bell. Their eyes met, each recognizing the direct challenge. Don Peters froze in fear at the idea of what might happen next. But Simpson just noted the event (albeit with some disgust) and continued to deal the cards, at which point Alan Dorfman fell out of his chair laughing and Peters allowed himself to exhale.

Eventually, Hamilton christened himself the Reverend Hampton.

Hampton because many of his black members mispronounced Hamilton as Hampton. Reverend because Hamilton and his fellow white business agents found black ministers to be a source of endless amusement. Because Hamilton was able to impersonate the cadence and the rhythm of the black gospel preachers well enough to amuse himself and others, he assumed the title of Reverend as an insider's dig at the "community"—another one of his favorite words.

The sexism at Local 743 was no less overt. Although it was progressive of Local 743 to have women in nonclerical positions, in the male testosterone contest that passed for an organizational chart, Regina was initially regarded as one of Bob Simpson's "girls."

For his part, Simpson had been right and wrong about his new recruit. Regina was kind of a hippie, as he had first thought. But not the drug-hazed, love-in kind. She was an idealist. An independent-minded feminist. An ideological humanist. In short, someone who Simpson, a dominating man known for his iron-handed control over others, particularly women, would have a hard time influencing let alone controlling or containing. And the capable, passionate, energetic, educated, articulate, and stubborn young woman was so unlike anyone else at Local 743 that she instantly became an object of jealousy and mistrust among the other "girls."

It must have pained Regina, a young woman dedicated to elevating the conditions of women, to discover that most of her sisters at the brotherhood were as out of touch as the men—and equally as threatened by her!

From childhood, Regina had learned to ignore her detractors in order to concentrate on those she needed to save. And whether or not she was popular among her immediate peers, she was thrilled to be playing on the team of what she saw as simply those who were working for what was right. So despite the racial and gender tensions within the local, Regina was extremely proud of 743's work for civil as well as worker rights and eager to organize women who needed her. According to Hamilton's son, Tom, Regina even ignored threats to her person that included a desire to "throw her white bitch ass out the window."

Blue Cross/Blue Shield

$\mathcal{W}$hile dodging knives aimed at her back, and ignoring her status at the office as anybody's "girl," Regina managed to find two friends and allies at Local 743 almost immediately.

Vicki Saporta, today president and CEO of the National Abortion Federation, was a kindred spirit. An idealistic and capable young woman in the process of distinguishing herself as a leader in the labor movement, she was sent to Chicago from international on a six-month assignment to help with the Blue Cross/Blue Shield campaign. She had begun her career as a representative for the Western Conference of Teamsters and would eventually become the first woman to serve as an organizing director for an international union.

While there were a large number of organizers working that campaign, Vicki was someone on Regina's team that she could relate to and trust. She too was young, white, female, feminist, passionate, and educated. Saporta's feelings about her tenure in Chicago's Local 743 are mixed.

"There was lots of drama in that particular local that was not necessarily typical of all Teamster local unions," says Saporta. "But we did it because there was nothing more fulfilling than organizing workers. Empowering people to make a difference in their lives was intoxicating. It was only when you had to deal with union politics that you started to wonder, *What am I doing and why am I doing it?* But the answer was, we thought that the Teamsters Union was the organization that had the greatest potential to do the greatest good for union people. So we put up with sexual harassment and a hostile working environment."

Vicki was the senior and more seasoned veteran of organizing, but Regina rose to the occasion quickly as the two surpassed the expectations established by Muriel Carroll and Clara Day, the more senior women organizers. Together, Vicki and Regina taught each other the intricacies of selling the concept of a union to workers while avoiding as many of the pitfalls of working in an aggressively male-dominated world as possible.

According to Paul Booth, today the executive assistant to the president of the American Federation of State, County and Municipal Employees and then cutting his teeth working with Chicago trade unions, "Local 743 at the time was an unreconstructed male world that had the anomaly of these two women that came to the challenge of union organizing by different paths and were superstars around the same time."

Along with 743's Muriel Carroll, the lead organizer and business agent, and Clara Day, a black woman who had marched with Peters in Washington in the '60s and was, by the time Regina met her, the first and only female trustee at Local 743, Vicki and Regina went to Blue Cross almost every day. "We had to be able to listen well and relate to the women we were talking to," says Saporta. "The women there were in a setting where they had their jobs but faced the same kinds of issues in any large workplace in terms of fairness and supervisory issues and those kinds of things."

The women at Blue Cross/Blue Shield were also somewhat inaccessible. In order to meet them, the women of Local 743 did a lot of entertaining. "Our big breakthrough came from hosting lunch hours in some eatery," recalls Saporta, "where Regina and I worked the room. We made major strides there."

Regina's other new friend and early mentor was Joel D'Alba, the attorney who had filed her unfair labor practice charge against the Red Star Inn. D'Alba would come to strategize with Regina on every major union campaign as well as numerous grievances. "We held most of our meetings at the Drake Hotel," D'Alba recalls. "Drinking tea and poring over grievances. She thought those teas were the height of civility."

With the brotherhood on one side and her more enlightened comrades on the other, Regina began oscillating between civility and incivility on a fairly regular basis.

With Vicki, she faced the coarseness and danger of picket lines, the heady sense of empowering other women, covert meetings at night, and pointed discourteousness by some of her Teamster brethren. With D'Alba, she strategized and studied in the tea room at the Drake Hotel—and began to acquire two sets of wardrobes for the disparate stages on which she performed.

In September of 1976 she wrote a report to the Central States Conference that captured the essence of what unions were up against in organizing the white-collar worker. "Whether we like it or not," she wrote, "clerical workers continue to cling to an image of themselves which is different from that of blue-collar workers. Though conditions and wages speak to the contrary, these workers conceive of themselves as 'middle class' rather than 'working class.' A clerical worker can be in a job that is less skilled and pays less than a warehouseman, yet still feel 'superior' in the office setting."

For this "status-conscious" and "image-conscious" group of women to consider "joining what is popularly conceived of as 'a truck drivers union,'" she wrote, "seems, to many, simply unpalatable. We hear it often: 'What do truck drivers know about data processors and claims adjusters?'"

Acknowledging that "the image of strength and old-fashioned clout that have come to be associated with Teamsters have served it well," she went on to say that white-collar women need other women—women who are conversant with their situations on the job as well as someone they can identify with psychologically—to feel secure joining the Teamsters. And she offered herself in the form of that security.

Despite her opponents, Regina's fervor for the union cause knew no boundaries and eventually earned her the respect and love of the man who would become her greatest friend and mentor, Ray Hamilton. "I think my dad was indifferent to Regina initially. She was white collar. His people were machinists and warehousemen. But somewhere around 1976, something about her triggered his change in attitude. He stopped seeing her as Simpson's girl and began to see her as the sharp, committed unionist that she was."

By that time, Regina was well on her way to stepping out from under Simpson's shadow. In 1976 she wrote a groundbreaking resolution—the first of its kind concerning women workers—that was endorsed by her local and adopted at the 21st Convention of the International Brotherhood of Teamsters.

In addition to her intelligence and commitment, Regina's sheer bravery contributed to the change in Ray Hamilton's attitude toward her. On one occasion, she was driving down a rural road at night in Cook County. Approaching the Diesel Recon Company, she noticed six men carrying homemade pickets out in front. "She stopped her car," D'Alba recalls of the incident, "explained who she was and what the Teamsters could do for them and signed them up on the spot. She later negotiated their contract, securing their business and Hamilton's lasting loyalty."

On another occasion, Regina chased an eighteen-wheeler truck whose driver had tried unsuccessfully to cross one of her picket lines. With angry Regina in hot pursuit, the driver eventually stopped the truck, got out of the cabin, and ran away from her on foot. Regina got out of her car as well and chased him into a bar, where she found him trying to make a phone call. Unbelievably, she presented her case and convinced the truck driver not to try and break the strike.

"Regina was a very aggressive people-type person," says Simpson in an even tone that conveys admiration. "She was a real fighter. In some instances, she was a lot more aggressive than I was." High praise from a man who, even in retirement 30 years after meeting her, exudes an alpha male quality that is as physically intimidating as his soft-spoken words are no-nonsense.

Yet, as Regina learned the tools of organizing, she began chafing at Bob Simpson's control over her actions and curtailment of her abilities. "Simpson physically threatened her," Hamilton's son Tom recalls. "He said something about throwing her white bitch ass out the window and he was the kind of guy you would assume would whack a woman."

Threats, however, are not actions. Regina wasn't intimidated by her tough-talking boss, and Simpson knew that as well as anyone. After all, it was her fearlessness that interested Simpson in the first place. But as time went on, she and Simpson continued to clash as she and Hamilton continued to bond.

And no matter what she may have felt personally about office theatrics, Regina stayed focused on her goal: organizing the women at Blue Cross/Blue Shield. It was a difficult campaign. So difficult that Don Peters devised a unique commission structure to incentivize his sales force. But despite the incentives, there were setbacks.

The Teamsters lost a close election for the unit of 1,500 Blue Cross/Blue Shield employees. But the union filed charges against the company and the National Labor Relations Board ordered a new election in which the union won.

After that victory, which neither Regina nor Vicki were credited with sealing, Vicki moved on. "I felt bad leaving her there when I left," says Saporta. "But we kept in touch. She was so excited when I got promoted to director of organizing. And we saw each other. I brought her in as a speaker at a labor conference for women. I stayed at her house."

There was no need to cry for Regina, however. With Simpson, Peters, Hamilton, and D'Alba stacked firmly behind her, she embarked next on the project that would seal her own fame as a labor organizer.

International Brotherhood of Teamsters Resolution on Women Workers

By Regina Polk, 1976

*W*omen are entering the labor force in ever increasing numbers. They now comprise more than 40% of the labor force. In spite of these ever growing numbers, almost 80% of women who work do not have the protection of a union contract.

Thus, these women suffer not only from the traditional ill conditions and low wages which male workers suffered some 30 years ago, and for which organized labor has vigilantly sought solutions, but they also suffer the added burden of discrimination in the workplace. The lack of union representation deprives these women workers of one of the most effective deterrents against discrimination on the job: a collective bargaining agreement.

Women continue to remain concentrated in two of the largest unorganized sectors of the economy, the service and clerical sectors. These areas are also among those which will experience the largest growth over the next decade. This means that the greatest opportunity for increasing the ranks of organized labor over the next decade lies with women workers.

The International Brotherhood of Teamsters has been in the forefront of the campaign to organize women workers, resulting in its status as the International Union with the largest number of women members. Thus, we have the tools and the experience to deliver the fruits and protections of organized labor to the bulk of women workers in the 1970s.

This achievement shall stand next to the I.B. of T.'s pioneering efforts to bring ever increasing numbers of minorities under collective bargaining agreements, as a crucial step in the struggle for a free and egalitarian society.

THEREFORE, the Teamsters Women's Council calls upon the International Brotherhood of Teamsters to:

1. Launch an intensive national organizing campaign directed at those areas of the labor force in which women are concentrated.

2. Work for equal opportunity on the job, whereby the collective bargaining agreement shall be the means of dealing the death blows to the employers' tools of discrimination (i.e., wage differentials based on sex, dual seniority lists, etc.).

3. Express acknowledgment and appreciation of the valuable contributions of Teamster women over the years.

4. Promote greater participation of women members at every level of the International Brotherhood of Teamsters.

5. Organize area conferences of Teamster women to be held within the next twelve (12) months for the purpose of developing programs to implement this resolution; representatives from these area conferences to then convene for a national conference.

✎ The University of Chicago

████████████████████████████

*I*n 1978 Don Peters got a call from the University of Chicago Hospital clerical workers expressing an interest in union representation. The University of Chicago, Peters knew, would be a tough nut. University of Chicago president Hannah Gray was famous for getting the union out at her previous employer—Yale University. The battle would be uphill.

A team of organizers was deployed to organize the hospital clerical workers including 28-year-old Blue Cross/Blue Shield–experienced Regina Polk. It was her first opportunity to get involved in a campaign from the very beginning.

Local 743 president Don Peters sweetened the pot once again by offering a bonus for organizing. "You gotta remember," he told his basically low-paid organizers, "there's a fin on each ankle," meaning that organizers would receive a five-dollar bonus for each card signed in favor of the union.

By then, Regina's experience had grown to meet her passion. She had learned a lot from Simpson, Saporta, and D'Alba while slowly securing the admiration and support of Hamilton. By then, she also anticipated the difficulties. The tedium. And even the potential dangers. But most importantly, she believed in herself and her cause—she had no interest in nor need of a "fin on each ankle."

In *Confessions of a Union Buster*, author Martin Jay Levitt describes what it takes to be a union organizer:

> I realized that organizing was going to take a lot more than clever tricks. It would require a kind of miracle worker to round up workers from the bottom of the economic and social barrel—people who were frightened, isolated, vulnerable—and turn them into a united force willing to do battle with rich and powerful corporations. It would be a job that never ended, a job that could consume one's life. I worked magic, not miracles, and I wanted out. I may have had the guts for organizing, I surely had the brain, but I didn't have the heart. . . . I hadn't expected to be down in the trenches with laundry women and bellhops.

Regina had all of the above including a heart. She exuded an active compassion for workers at the bottom of the economic and social barrel. The same compassion she had expressed on the farm toward her beloved animals.

As a warrior, Regina was exhilarated in her fight for the hospital clerical workers against the rich and powerful corporation. She was brazen and unapologetic when personally threatened or harassed. When the University of Chicago management saw her as trespassing on their property, it was a non-issue. She was too busy pounding on doors and making thousands of phone calls to concern herself with their limitations. Needless to say, she wasn't worried about her own safety. She was concerned about the workers. She knew from personal experience that employers frequently try to get rid of workers who want a union. And she knew that even after the cards were signed, she would have to live with the workers who trusted her for 45 anxiety-ridden days before the election. Workers who would be threatened and harassed. Workers who were scared.

But when Regina said, "We are the Teamsters and we want to represent you. We can get contracts for you. Contracts that will be better than what you are living with now—if you have one at all," people sensed her sincerity and trusted her strength.

Still, fearful of trusting a union tainted by highly publicized criminal circuses on a national level that included arrests and convictions of union leaders for conspiracy, wire fraud, jury tampering, and a host of other illegal activities, the women challenged Regina. They questioned her about the national scandals. They questioned her about rumors that Don Peters and Local 743 were connected with the mob.

A loyal team player, a feminist, and a true unionist, Regina listened to the accusations against her union and her boss. She defended the union by pointing out the good it had done for its members. She defended Peters by using his own track record of accomplishments. And she championed Local 743 by telling the hospital workers (many of whom were black women) how Peters had organized marginalized people—black women, for instance, who nobody had organized before and most Teamster locals wouldn't touch. She talked about the delegation from Local 743 at the 1963 civil rights march on Washington. She expressed her heartfelt beliefs, and eventually her sincerity convinced the workers of her belief in Peters, in the union, and in them.

"It was amazing how she handled employees," says former union steward Maggie Newman. "Very simply, she told us, 'I am here today and I'll be here tomorrow. You tell me what your problems are and I'm going to try to help solve them.' She inspired a great loyalty."

She cared deeply. The women Regina talked to needed a voice and she became that voice. Her goal was to empower the women she was organizing, give them a sense of mission, and help them to pull it off. She was accessible. Regularly, she sat on the University of Chicago Quad waiting for people to come talk to her. She emphasized that women should remember that their close personal relationships with their bosses and management affiliations should not take precedence over their own needs. As a result of her efforts and sincerity, she gained a strong following among hospital clericals and secured more than enough signed cards expressing an interest in joining the union. Then the university threw a curveball.

When the union presented the National Labor Relations Board with a petition to hold an election, the university asked that the entire university—hospital *and* university clericals—be included in the vote.

"They did this because they believed the hospital side was a shoo-in for the union," explains Maggie Newman, "while the campus side would be traditionally pro-management. And this was true to a point. But what they [management] failed to figure out was that the campus clericals were so disillusioned and so underpaid in every way."

The University of Chicago had long been faculty dominated. Each department had its own hierarchy, its own rules and policies, and a wide range of job descriptions created idiosyncratically by each department. And while there was a personnel department (now called human resources) that was required to approve the job descriptions, the faculty was dominant. In departments that were well funded, people were paid better. In academic departments without a lot of money, the clericals were not paid well.

The university's labor relations staff also failed to realize the power of Regina Polk's commitment to stand behind every person she organized. She wasn't in it for the "fin on every ankle" that was offered as an incentive. Because of her relationship with Tom Heagy, her life was more financially comfortable than anyone else's on her team would ever be. But she never forgot that the people who signed those cards—people with families who needed their income—were putting their jobs on the line with their signature and she took care of them. Often, she was called out in the middle of the night—when it was safe to talk. And she listened . . . and listened . . . and listened.

Some of what she heard was almost comical. For example, in an effort to do damage control, the university sent representatives from personnel to meet with workers to discuss salary increases. When the representative met with library workers and pulled out the chart showing salary ranges, the library workers were stunned. Unbeknownst to personnel, the library managers had simply taken correction fluid and obscured the upper range in each pay category. The meeting with the personnel representative was the first time workers ever saw the upper-range salaries. They were stunned first and then empowered to sign the union cards.

"The library was one of the most exploited of departments," says Maggie Newman. "The whiting out of pay scales is typical. They would hire people who had complete knowledge of the Dewey decimal system and the Library of Congress cataloging system and were fluent in three languages and they got them by exploiting the hell out of grad students and paying them zip."

Union steward Edna Hunter describes Regina's organizing strategy at the university as covert. "We went underground," she recalls. "It was a unique group of organizers in that it comprised people able to keep their mouths closed. Also, we were conveying a different image. She loved Jimmy Hoffa but to organize the University of Chicago, you don't just go in and threaten the dean!"

As the campaign heated up, Regina made enemies. Not with the University of Chicago management, as one might expect, but within her own brotherhood. She was promoted to head the campaign and one by one the knives came out once again. The women who were older, more experienced, and not as successful remained jealous. They wanted the "fin on each ankle." They wanted the power. And many of the men at Local 743 believed that Regina was moving too fast.

"I think that it was because she was so aggressive," says Simpson, "but I can remember specifically one guy saying to me, 'I didn't like her from fuckin' day one!' And that was exactly his words and this guy was a board member."

Echoing Simpson's recollection, Joel D'Alba remembers that the then-joint council president Louis Pieck hated Regina because of her increasing influence in Local 743. "He felt that a woman should not have that kind of influence in the Teamsters Union," said D'Alba. "But Regina picked up on what Don Peters had started—she spent lots of time and energy that others didn't."

"She was an atypical union organizer and heavy-duty Teamster at a local who was successful at organizing, bargaining, and representing at a time when a lot of women weren't doing that," says Vicki Saporta. "And so there were conflicts internally as well as externally."

There were also rivalries. "People would get jealous over Gina's attention," recalls Newman. "People would compete for her. And Ray was used to being her go-to guy so if he had the slightest inkling that she was confiding in one of us or agreed with one of us he would get real snarky."

Newman was not one of Hamilton's biggest fans. "He was into 'Buy America'," remembers Maggie Newman, "and criticized me for ordering imported beer! I said American jobs aren't sacred. A brewery worker is a brewery worker, but for him it was all about America."

Regina persevered, keeping Hamilton as well as Newman as intimates. And as far as some of her detractors were concerned, she wasn't doing what she was doing to make office chums—even among her beloved brotherhood. She had too much work to do to think about petty rivalries. She got her cards signed and increasingly depended on Hamilton for support.

Finally, in October of 1979, the bitterly fought campaign resulted in a union victory by a vote of 712 to 706 with 87 challenged ballots. The university was stunned. It had failed to realize that over the previous 20 years the people who worked on campus were no longer faculty wives but bread-winners who needed the money. They were mothers, many of them single, whose paltry paychecks started looking worse and worse.

Thrilled with abilities that he felt matched his own, union president Don Peters recalled, "Regina and I would meet almost every day to talk about the challenges. We discussed whether each challenged voter was pro-union or anti-union. Over a period of time we agreed on which challenges we would accept and which ones we would oppose."

After months of wrangling between the university and the union, both parties agreed to count 37 ballots. Five months after the election, the National Labor Relations Board declared the union a winner by a vote of 743 to 722. Although the union had technically only squeaked by in the election, it was a huge victory. Two thousand new Teamsters.

After the election victory, Regina worked with union president Don Peters and Bob Simpson on the first university contract. As servicing representative, she also stayed in close contact with the new members at the University of Chicago during the harrowing time between the election victory and contract agreement. Regularly she sat down next to the flagpole on the quadrangle at the University of Chicago campus to hold impromptu question-and-answer meetings, and members would come by to talk about their concerns and fears. Union steward Maggie Newman says, "She single-handedly turned people's heads around about what it meant to be in a union and to bargain with an employer. It was just remarkable."

Remarkable but very difficult, as she met with resistance from many of the newly unionized employees. A woman who had been the steward in the Graduate School of Business (a conservative department) was horrified at the effrontery of the clerical workers' demands and walked out of the very first meeting.

"Many of the stewards were actually anti-union and there to police the union," says Newman. "That's how my best friend first got on the committee. She wasn't pro-union and her boss told her to 'get on this committee and see what the union is up to.' Well, when she did, she decided that the union was up to good—and a big part of that was Gina. Meeting her, seeing her enthusiasm, hearing her stories."

Regina didn't lose any time in replacing dissenters with stewards committed to the union. "I was introduced to her by a political friend," says Maggie Newman. "I had just had a baby and the union won while I was on maternity leave. We had lunch and she told me that we had squeaked by in the election and that the university was stonewalling on bargaining. She wanted me to get right into the bargaining team even though I hadn't been elected a steward yet."

Like most people, Newman did not say no to Regina's passionate entreaty. "I was always just in awe of her," says Newman. "She just came onstage to me as this utterly classy, self-confident, kick-ass woman I was in her car once and there was a packet of some diet drink. I said, 'Gina, what are you doing with this?' And she said, 'Oh, it's for pouring in scabs' gas tanks.' And she said it so matter of factly. She was unafraid of confrontation."

Maggie describes the early bargaining meetings with the university as being thrown into the deep end of the pool. A mediator had already been brought in because the university was still so shaken that they didn't have a plan and were making lowball and stupid offers. "When we first went into negotiations, Regina was tireless. There were many late nights and meetings and meetings and meetings. She was determined to stay in touch with the membership. It was such a breath of fresh air to have somebody that accessible."

In addition to continual one-on-one meetings, to find out what the workers wanted in their contract, Regina would fill entire auditoriums.

"Gina won everybody over by being so well-informed, sincere, and genuine in her concern," continues Newman. "She would bring workers' stories from one department or sector to another. She was the one who told us that many of the employees were eligible for food stamps! Their income was that low! So she spread the word and made people aware of each other. She told us who was fired for being five minutes late or for taking a phone call. One woman was fired for taking a call saying that her husband had had a heart attack! There were real abuses going on and it was Gina who broke down barriers and made people aware that not everybody was as lucky as others."

"She was versatile," says Edna Hunter. "She could vacillate between all these roles. A union person that could talk about other things. Art. Clothes. And on our way to union meetings, she had a knack to make you feel good about yourself. Whenever she met you, she might say, 'You're happy and cheery today' or might compliment you on your clothes. She was tall and I'm tall and she would say, 'Edna you wear your clothes so gracefully.' She didn't talk much about herself. I think a warrior or person interested in helping everybody else doesn't focus on themselves. She was a rebel *with* a cause."

Although the faculty was outraged at having to share power with secretaries, the negotiating team became extremely attached to Regina because of her dedication and knowledge. Edna Hunter describes the dream team of Peters, Polk, and Simpson with admiration: "At that first negotiation, the union blew them out of the water. Regina looked like somebody from the suburbs but she was tough. Couldn't be corralled. Bob Simpson looked distinguished but like he could strong arm you if he had to. And Don Peters had a photogenic memory. As time went on, these people who worked at an institution of higher learning (people from human resources and a few administration VIPs from other areas) were impressed to the limit that Don could remember verbatim what had taken place two sessions back. He didn't even have to look at notes and tell you exactly what happened."

Asking for a 20 percent raise, a formal written grievance procedure, seniority rules for hiring and promotion, and a better benefits package, Regina had developed such loyalty that even dissenters changed their minds. According to Peters, "Through Regina's efforts, dedication, and loyalty, negotiating committee members who opposed the union shop switched and supported it. One day at 3 o'clock in the morning, one of the members admitted she had been working with management to sabotage the union. Over the period of negotiations, she changed her mind and said she would do everything possible to get a union shop, raises, and other benefits. That early morning meeting changed the complexion of negotiations."

As Regina's role shifted from organizer to negotiator, she began to dress for her audience the way an actress does. With the workers, she wore jeans to show solidarity. With management, she became the best dressed person in the room, complete with high heels and a hat. On those occasions, her costumes were designed not to show solidarity but superiority.

In both a generous and calculated move, Regina also began to dress the women on her team. "She gave me a green dress with tan suede trim," recalls Edna Hunter. "She said, 'I'm gonna give you this dress and you're gonna look better in it than me because you have more behind!'"

"She must have given me a dozen power suits," says Maggie Newman. "Jones of New York!"

Regina had figured out how to turn her passion for clothing into theatrical props. "She taught me that you intimidate people with those clothes," says Maggie Newman. "That if you're dressed as well as management it puts them off and your members see you as someone with power."

Robert W. McAllister was a neutral arbitrator assigned to resolve disputes between the union and the employers. He had profound respect for Regina. "Anyone who negotiates contracts has to be performance oriented," he explains. "We are all actors. And when you are negotiating on behalf of others, you better be a little bit of a chameleon."

"Regina was a dazzling breath of fresh air," says Newman. "After having this image of a heavy-set guy with a pinkie ring who drives a Cadillac, here comes this woman dressed in designer clothes with high heels and always looking fabulous who just goes in and kicks ass."

Despite the supreme efforts, negotiations reached an impasse. The university would not budge. And Regina began to express dissatisfaction with her local's refusal to confront them directly, immediately, and boldly.

"She talked of filing a lawsuit with the NLRB [National Labor Relations Board] for failure to bargain," says Newman. "She wanted to challenge the excessive delays that undermine the negotiating process but said that Peters and Simpson rejected the idea of doing something that would make the university too mad."

According to arbitrator Robert McAllister, "She was the most caring union official possible. She looked at those individuals who worked at the University of Chicago like a mother."

As a last resort, Regina helped convince the new members to do the only thing left to them to do: and a remarkable 87 percent voted their approval for a strike.

"Gina was [somehow] able to convey a message that we weren't really going to go on strike but we had to convince the university that we were willing to go on strike in order to get them to be serious," says Newman. "You can't say in so many words that you don't want to strike because you want them to believe that you will and yet want to assuage the fears of these people who don't want to go on strike. It has to be a credible threat."

Only then, with the threat of a strike hanging over their collective heads, did the University of Chicago's management begin to negotiate seriously. In an 11-hour session on October 29, 1979, a settlement was agreed upon and two weeks later, union members approved their first contract, by a vote of 962 to 90. The contract included the following provisions:

- All union members received an average salary increase of 23 percent over two years.
- Nine hundred thirty-two secretaries won a promotion to a higher pay grade with an additional raise of 40 cents an hour.
- A joint union-management committee was to be established to revise the classification system, seniority rights, and bumping rights.
- A short-term disability policy and a grievance procedure were to be put in place.

"Regina played a big role in overhauling the classification system by keeping us focused," says Newman. "She saw to it that we stuck together."

To celebrate their victory, the University of Chicago stewards threw Regina a surprise testimonial dinner at the Windermere Hotel, where they presented her with a gavel because she was always banging on the table to restore order. "It was an extraordinary first contract," says Newman. "And we got it by slugging our guts out, bargaining our asses off. It was an enormous amount of money and all those stewards were just so dizzy with satisfaction and delight and we owed it all to Gina."

Two years after the contract was ratified, the committee completely reformed the classification system and helped many clericals win pay increases. Most significantly, the contract's grievance procedure destroyed the system of favoritism, nepotism, and cronyism that favored political might over what was right at the university.

By the end of 1979, Regina's reputation for organizing and negotiating was firmly established. President Don Peters clearly saw a star in his young protégé and promoted the 29-year-old brainy and now influential beauty to business agent. As such, she was also eligible to run for office.

Her ability to handle the threatened strike and loyalty among the members was now a boon to Peters's empire, but at the same time it was also a threat.

"Don Peters was an old-time, traditional unionist and his wife was a very liberal lady, very instrumental in influencing Don to hire women," says arbitrator and attorney Robert McAllister. "Regina was an asset and a star but it was still a stunner when she became a business agent."

"You can imagine the thrill of this youngster to be promoted to this position," Regina's friend and mentor Ray Hamilton recollects. "But as we were celebrating the event—and there were lots of celebrations, every day about—she stopped in her happiness and anxiety and smiling and said, 'I must buy some new clothes!'

"And I said, well, you're always buying new clothes. And she said, 'No, this is a big problem. I've got to buy some clothes. I've gotta change my hair. Buy new shoes. I'm too young! The people won't listen to me. I can't lead them!'

"I said, 'What the hell are you talking about? I'm a hell of a lot older than them and you and you're always leading me around, so don't worry about leading. You can lead and don't worry about the clothes. What the hell, Joan of Arc didn't get a new armored suit when she took over. So don't worry about anything. Continue to lead.' And lead, she did."

♥ A Marriage of Equal Opposites

███████████████████████████████████

On April 12, 1980, surrounded by their parents, one of Tom's brothers, Eileen and Stan (married by then), Gina's nephew, Michael, and a host of friends, Thomas Heagy and Regina Polk stood side by side in a small Swedenborgian church in San Francisco. According to the teachings of Emanuel Swedenborg, all people who live good lives, no matter what their religion, have a place in heaven. At the time, the Heagys were actually only looking for a place near their families in San Francisco.

Gina wore a white lace dress and signature large hat covered by a veil. The beautiful and increasingly powerful Teamster giggled at the line "for richer and for poorer" because Tom had just lost all of his savings speculating on the British pound.

They weren't worried. They had found each other and their callings in life. Regina was a Teamster star by then and Tom was a very young chairman and CEO of the reform-renowned South Shore Bank. In addition to promising to love, honor, and cherish each other, they had a solid understanding. Tom would help and support his new wife in whatever way he could (including phone calls, picket line activity, and her frequent trips to shoe stores). In return, she would keep the union away from his bank.

"Tom must have felt that he had captured a bird of paradise and didn't know what to do with it because she was so flamboyant and gorgeous," recalls Maggie Newman. "And he just basked in her glow."

After a honeymoon spent cruising the Mediterranean, Tom kept his word and continued to hand out leaflets while advising Regina on how to convince arbitrators and management during negotiations. Acknowledging his unique privilege of being married to a union organizer and business agent, Tom developed an appreciation of cooperation between labor and management. "To quote a union buster," Tom says, "you only get a union if you deserve one."

"She had as much power as Tom," says Amy Burack, who attended the wedding with her future husband, Tom's friend Michael. "It was an equal relationship but not based on money. She was committed to the cause and he loved that side of her."

Their life together was unusual. They worked in different worlds, had many separate friends, and yet thoroughly enjoyed each other and the kind of comfort that money can buy.

As the wife of a successful banker, Regina was able to increasingly enjoy travel, music, gourmet food, art collection, as many designer clothes as she liked, and enough shoes to be the envy of Imelda Marcos. She became a supporter of the University of Chicago's Renaissance Society as well as an accomplished hostess, throwing elaborate dinner parties that she cooked herself, often with the aid of *Gourmet Magazine*.

As the husband of a Teamster, Tom accepted long absences for meetings that took place late at night while looking after an ever-increasing brood of animals that Regina adored.

Despite her experience in a California jail, Gina continued to take her chances with the police and refused to put Morgan on a leash when the three of them went for walks in the evening.

"One night Gina was walking Morgan by herself," recalls Tom, "and Morgan was making unfriendly noises toward some guy on the street.

The guy told Gina, 'If your dog comes near me I'll shoot him.' Gina's cool response? 'If you shoot my dog I'll shoot you.' Gina wasn't about to be bullied.

"Morgan ran away once," says Tom, remembering a time when Gina *was* afraid. "I went to the pound to try to find him and discovered that there was more than one pound. Each animal rescue has its own place, and I went to about three of them before finding Morgan on the floor, totally miserable. As soon as he saw me he was very excited. I think it was the happiest anyone has been to see me in my entire life. Gina was ecstatic. She didn't think that we would find him."

On another occasion, Regina "adopted" a kitten named Flower to keep their cat Stanley company. "She came home one day with something in her handbag," says Tom. "She was holding it up in the air and Morgan was jumping and sniffing and I thought it was a hamburger. Then I see this little tiny kitten stick its face out of the bag. 'What's that?' I asked."

Regina explained to Tom at the time that she was driving down the Dan Ryan, saw the cat in a culvert, and pulled over to save it. "But," recalls Tom, "a couple of months later we were at a party and one of her union friends asked, 'How's that kitten I gave you?' and I realized that the whole story had been implausible. It was all right. I had gotten used to the cat. I was irritated . . . but not too."

When Morgan died of cancer, it was very hard on Regina. "I still remember the vet calling to say they had opened him up but there was nothing they could do," recalls Tom.

Regina, however, figured out something to do. Mirroring the adoption of Flower, Regina neglected to include Tom in the decision and showed up one day with an aloof rabbit, which she had named Peter (first name) Rabbit (surname).

"The rabbit was a mistake," Tom says now. "Regina had heard that they make wonderful pets but this one was sick all the time and needed a lot of care."

In addition to the rabbit's illness, its name continued to be a problem.

At the pharmacy, Tom would whisper, "I am picking up a prescription. Rabbit is the last name."

"I don't see it," said the pharmacist. "What's the first name?

Tom whispered, "Peter."

"Is this a rabbit?"

Barely audible, "Yes."

"Last name of the owner!"

"Heagy."

"Here it is. Peter Heagy."

It is apparently difficult to determine the sex of a young rabbit. Several vet trips into their relationship, the Heagy-Polks were told that Peter was a female. Renamed Emily, the rabbit was no more enjoyable or adorable than she had been while going through life as a male. "Regina thought it was going to be cuddly and it wasn't cuddly," says Tom with a wry smile. "It wanted to eat and be left alone."

Not completely alone, however. One day Tom and Gina came home to find Emily humping Flower and discovered that it was male after all. Still aloof and sickly, but male and cross-species-sexual. "I had that rabbit for five years," says Tom. "Two with her and three on my own."

"I've always wondered why she didn't go into animal rights," says her friend Shelley Carter. "Her love of animals was unconditional in a way that she couldn't do with people. Yet, labor gave her the opportunity to give as much as she could in terms of human rights."

"She was a great animal lover and loved to fight with my ex-husband Michael," says Amy Burack. The fights were especially heated in restaurants that served rabbit on the menu. "Michael was a bit of a provocateur," recalls Amy. "He would ask the waiter how the rabbit was prepared just to get her mad. Sometimes they went a little far."

If verbal descriptions of braised, wrapped, shredded, and bundled bunny loin were painful to Regina, they must have paled in comparison to what she wanted to do to Michael. Tom, however, supported her in whatever she deemed necessary. In addition to avoiding bunny meals, he continued to walk picket lines, make phone calls, and tolerate frequent absences, late nights, and even an ice pick (in addition to the diet powder) in their glove compartment. "She needed it on picket lines," he explains simply. "To slash tires. Although," he corrects himself for accuracy, "technically, the tires don't get slashed, they get punctured."

Commenting on Regina's aggressive side, Bob Simpson speaks proudly of the woman he couldn't control, "She was a strong Teamster and that's different than other unions."

"She revered Jimmy Hoffa," explains Tom. "She romanticized that old-style Teamster stuff, which she saw as clear good against evil as opposed to all of the legal complications that she participated in."

While Regina would talk for hours about causes, her friends knew very little about the woman who demonstrated such care and compassion for others.

According to Tom's friend and fellow banker Sarah Brown, "Whenever you saw her, she was interested in what *you* were doing. She was a good listener. She would not talk about herself. You would have to question her to get information."

Amy Burack says, "She sparkled with excitement and mystery."

Local 743 attorney Joel D'Alba noted that Regina had the ability to go between the world of high culture and the street without missing a beat. "She would go to the opera dressed in her finest and discuss grievances with me over tea in the Drake Hotel. But she had the guts of a street fighter."

Regina's picket-line activities led to many charges being filed against her for misconduct. Robert Simpson recalls an episode not long after her wedding in which Regina slapped a policeman:

> There was a strike on Mannheim Road in Rosemont because the company was trying to get rid of the union. Now the police in that area were very anti-union and didn't cut us no slack. A truck tried to cross our picket line but we had picketers in the driveway to keep that from happening. It was a continuous line with no

break. Anyway, the police came up and told us to get out of the driveway or they would move us out. One of them put his hands on Regina to make her move and called her a bitch. Well, she called him a pig and slapped the shit out of him.

She got arrested for assaulting a police officer, a class X felony, a minimum of one year in jail. But the union exercised all of its power to keep her out of jail. They couldn't influence judges or city officials but Ray Hamilton allegedly made a deal with the cop to get him a job through the union in exchange for dropping the charges.

"I thought it was a major accomplishment that she was so gutsy," marvels Sarah Brown. "Her appearance was such that you thought she would never hit a policeman but she was very fiery when she needed to be."

Bob Simpson was also of the "do whatever it takes" philosophy. "On that same strike, to stop a truck I let it bump me and then I fell out in the street," he recalls. "This racist cop came over and screamed everything at me that he could think of. The ambulance came and put me on stretcher and this guy is still screaming and yelling. 'Bring Jesse Jackson out here, you black bastard,' et cetera. Finally, the ambulance driver found something wrong with my pulse and told him to leave me alone. The cop took my license. I got hit by the truck and he took *my* license! Again, I called Peters and he got my license back. Somehow."

After a subsequent arrest in Cook County, Regina was told to put her wallet on the desk. She did as she was told but asked for a receipt. The extremely large policewoman told her in no uncertain terms that she would not be getting a receipt but offered to wipe her "white ass all over the floor." At that point, Regina decided that a receipt would be unnecessary.

"Working for the union taught me not to be afraid of a policeman," says Simpson. "I had no problem telling them to fuck off. In fact, I had the captain of the police labor detail go to Don Peters many times [to complain]. But they make you act like that. Regina was pretty aggressive on the picket lines, but I could understand very well why she acted the way she did. They treat you like you're dirt and have no rights. We know our rights. But city policemen weren't as up to snuff as the guys from the labor detail. They knew we had a right to stop trucks and talk to them. City policemen figured we had no right."

Sarah Brown laughs lovingly at the memories of Regina calling Tom at the bank from jail. "I'm in again," she would say. "Josephs?" Tom replied, thinking that Regina's shoe fetish had got the better of her again. "Not Josephs," Regina would laugh. "Jail!"

According to her friend and Local 743 attorney Joel D'Alba, "Regina often had charges filed against her for picket-line misconduct during strikes as well as charges by police officers of her throwing coffee at them."

Gina yearned for the good old days when things were more violent but simpler and traditional confrontational unionism was the norm. Perhaps it was from growing up with a Western shoot-'em-up ethos. When she recognized underhanded maneuvers on the part of management—such as the practice of hiring off-duty police officers to moonlight as "security" with all of the powers of police officers—Gina publicly insisted that, "management still has goons, only now they call them police."

But not even Tom worried too much about Regina's behavior. She and D'Alba had a strategy that worked repeatedly. Each time she was accused of picket-line misconduct, Regina would appear before the court dressed as demurely as possible in a beautiful dress and hat. According to D'Alba, nobody would believe that such an attractive and well-dressed woman could do the things she was alleged to have done.

Tom recalls "an apocryphal story that Gina liked to tell":

> A union guy and a management guy confront each
> other in front of a picket line. The management guy
> says, "I drop my handkerchief and twenty guys come

out of that truck." The union guy counters, "I take off my glasses and two sticks of dynamite blow up the truck."

As Regina and Ray Hamilton's relationship blossomed through work, she and Tom socialized frequently with the Hamilton family despite their disparate interests. "Tom Heagy was perhaps as brilliant as anyone I ever met," says Hamilton's son Tom. "No subject was off limits. I remember my dad inviting Tom to a Notre Dame football game on a 95-degree early September day. My brothers and I were sitting in a different part of the open bowl stadium. It was tough for us—and we loved Notre Dame football. It had to be torture for Tom, who could have been somewhere thinking great thoughts."

The Heagys would reciprocate by taking the Hamiltons to the Chicago Symphony Orchestra. "Surprisingly," says Tom Hamilton, "my dad rather enjoyed it."

The foursome also frequented restaurants. Gourmet when it was the Heagys' turn to pick. More pedestrian when it was the Hamiltons'.

"The Heagys would take my parents to a place like Gordon's," recalls Tom. "My parents would reciprocate by taking them to a place like Comeback Inn in Melrose Park, where Regina wouldn't even touch the food." She was a Teamster for sure but also an epicurean and loved keeping a foot in each of her different worlds—especially when the foot was clad in a delicate heel and the food was enhanced by a reduction sauce.

They met in an economics class and went to a flute concert for their first date.

Regina and Tom, 1980.

The Heagys and the Polks at Tom and Regina's wedding, 1980.

Sweet love.

☙ Governors State/Chicago State

███████████████████████████████████

$\mathcal{W}$hile she stayed in close contact with the new members she had organized at the University of Chicago, Regina's next assignment—and first one as a business agent—was twofold:

- to negotiate a contract for the already unionized Chicago State
- to organize and act as business agent for a 150-employee clerical unit at Governors State University

Regina worked closely on both campaigns with Ray Hamilton, whose mentoring and friendship would turn out to be the equivalent of doctoral work in how to be a Teamster—despite her finicky eating habits. According to Simpson, "He helped Regina a lot. She was still new as a business agent and there was a lot of stuff she didn't know."

And there was a lot to know. The Illinois State Board of Governors oversaw five schools: Eastern Illinois, Western Illinois, Governors State University, Chicago State University, and Northeastern Illinois University. Unlike the privately held University of Chicago, these schools were governed by a public bureaucracy and presented an entirely different set of challenges.

Ray Kujawa was the union steward at Chicago State University. "I was used to doing whatever I wanted to do," he recalls of his early days as a steward. "I came in early and left early. When Regina took over, my life changed dramatically. The first time I heard from her she called a meeting for 5 o'clock in the afternoon! I wasn't happy. I was going to have to come back to work."

Kujawa changed his mind about the aggressive young woman immediately. "The moment I met her, I fell in love with her. She was so stunning. A knockout. She looked like Sharon Stone. But she had big balls for a lady. She would take over places, just walk past management."

Kujawa came to love and respect Regina so much that he worked harder for her than he had ever worked before. "Our relationship was very close. She was probably the most intelligent person I have ever met in my life."

With Regina at the helm, everybody worked harder than they had ever worked before. She called continuous meetings and constantly created new questionnaires asking members what they wanted to see in their new contract. She worked all day and often late into the night gathering the information she needed about her members. As steward, Kujawa was an integral partner, serving as the middleman between the workers, the management, and the union, and he spent many late nights at Gina's meetings. "She had very little regard for her own life and her own safety," Kujawa remembers. "We would be leaving to go home at night and I wanted to walk her to the car. 'Don't bother, I'm fine' she'd say. 'Don't worry about me.'"

She frequently held meetings in her home as well. Meetings that went late. Meetings that revealed the dichotomy between her salary and her lifestyle to people who weren't used to the good life.

"She'd call Edwardo's Pizza in Hyde Park, order a $30 pizza, and tip the delivery boy ten bucks!" Kujawa remembers. "We were making about two bucks an hour back then."

At the negotiating table, Regina would transform herself and her style of negotiations to match the style of the person across the table— a style that baffled management and eventually broke their resistance.

"She could have a 'little girl' look or be extremely sophisticated," says Kujawa. "Once, when the university was playing hardball, five of us were still sitting around a table at 2 o'clock in the morning: the board negotiator, someone from human resources, Regina, myself, and somebody else. And the woman from human resources finally said, 'I'm just so tired I'm gonna give you what you want, okay?'

"I said, 'That's really nice,' and Regina punched me hard on the arm and said, 'Don't you ever say anything like that in a negotiation again!' For her, they weren't *giving* us anything. We earned it. The members deserved it. And she could go for as many hours as it took to fight for the contract. 'Quitting is the easy thing to do,' she used to tell us."

The hard work and late nights paid off. In 1980 Regina negotiated her first contract at Chicago State, which resulted in substantial wage increases and a lot more. She was so well versed by then in the State University Merit Classification System that she convinced the Merit Commission to audit the positions in the bargaining unit and many people got upgrades.

That contract also contained groundbreaking language on video display terminals (VDTs), the forerunner of modern-day computers— language that required the university to grant employees who worked continuously on VDTs or other similar equipment additional breaks during the workday. This language remains unchanged some 24 years after Regina negotiated it into the contract.

"She was very good at putting language into contracts and convincing university management that this was good for both sides," says Kujawa. "She was able to talk people into agreeing to items that I thought we would never get into a contract."

By then, as a result of her success at the University of Chicago, Regina was being recognized on a national level in publications as significant as *Time* magazine and the *New York Times*. The September 15, 1980, issue of *Time* reported:

> As inflation reduces real incomes and recession erodes job security, office employees are starting to look for a union label. Says Teamster Organizer Regina Polk: "The white-collar worker is coming around to realizing that while he is enjoying titles and so-called professionalism, the guy in the warehouse is earning more."

While working on Chicago State's new contract, Regina simultaneously began organizing the clerical workers at Governors State University. At the first organizing meeting where employees were asked to sign cards for the union, a petite woman named Phyllis Bacon spoke out in favor of the union. "My mother was a labor supporter and walked picket lines," Bacon explains. "So that was ingrained in me."

With that, Bacon caught Regina's attention and Regina quickly convinced Bacon to serve on the organizing committee.

As time went by, one by one the women signed Regina's cards and began the slow process of learning how to fight for themselves. "Women were learning how to be men," says Bacon. "Labor always had a good-old-boys reputation, but Regina brought labor to women by standing behind us, in front of us, and at our sides. She was a fighter and she taught me how to fight—fairly and professionally."

During the organizing (and later, the contract negotiations), Regina spent night after night at Bacon's house. Strategizing. Thinking. Writing contracts. Eating pizza. "Regina taught us that it was all about selective pressure," says Bacon, who even scored a free midnight makeover.

"One night she said to me, 'You're a plain Jane, Phyllis—let's get your makeup and see what we can do.' We were just workers but we knew we were loved. She put us before herself. She always put *you* first. She had buttons made that read '59 Cents,'" remembers Bacon, "because women made 59 cents to a man's dollar."

"She was so committed to making people's lives better," says Regina's sister, Eileen. "Especially for women. She had this burning desire to make the world right in terms of equality for the sexes."

The union won the election overwhelmingly at Governors State but Regina, once again, didn't stop strategizing for a second.

"We were talking," recalls Bacon, "and she said, 'Now as a member of the negotiating committee . . .,' and I cut her off and told her I didn't want to do it! My job was important and the campaign was a lot of work. But with Regina, you're just not done. She was so sincere that you really could not say no to her because she inspired loyalty and believed in you."

It would have been hard for anyone to complain about working too hard to Regina—a woman who was simultaneously juggling members at the University of Chicago, Chicago State, and Governors State. Phyllis wound up agreeing to join the negotiating committee.

Bacon shared Kujawa's concerns for Regina's safety. "She spent a lot of time away from her husband. After meetings that went late, I would urge her to at least call so he would know she was on her way but she didn't want to bother him. 'What difference does it make?' she'd ask. 'What can he do? I'm not worried. And whatever is going to happen is going to happen anyway.'"

Ray Hamilton's son Tom spent a good deal of time with Regina as well. While Regina was learning the intricacies of negotiating from Ray Hamilton, she was apparently happy to share her experiences with his still college-age son, who was interested in the labor movement mostly out of admiration for his father. "The things that remain most permanently ingrained in my memory are the disconnects," the younger Hamilton remembers, adding an interesting and important dimension to Regina's character. "The incongruities and inconsistencies. She was always extremely nice to me, but looking back on it and even then, there were so many contradictions in words as well as actions. She loved John Travolta in *Urban Cowboy*, the blue-collar workers who she admired as the salt-of-the-earth working people. On the other hand, there was the never-ending parade of clothes, shoes, sunglasses, and handbags. Even when I was a 19-year-old kid who knew nothing of women's fashion, I recall thinking, 'Damn, that outfit looks expensive.'"

On a couple of occasions when Tom Hamilton was at DePaul University, Regina invited him to breakfast at Lou Mitchell's. "She would sit there and drink cup after cup of coffee," he muses, "while I missed classes. We would meet at 7 A.M. I would have an 8:30 A.M. class. We'd end up leaving at 10:30. Our breakfasts and lunches could go on for hours. I still marvel that she acted as though she had all the time in the world for me."

"My daughter is a freshman in college today," Tom says "I occasionally drive her and her friends to Bloomington, so I have a sense of college-level conversation. I just can't see spending time with kids other than my own. They can be bright and funny, but we just don't have enough in common to keep things interesting for long. If someone told me that I would have to spend time with some college kid showing him or her the ropes, I'd be nervous thinking how many phone calls were going unanswered and how much shit was building up on my desk. She never displayed any such anxiety. On the other hand, maybe she felt her most important duty was mentoring me. If so, she was amazingly more giving than I could ever be."

In addition to meals, Regina took Tom with her to union negotiations at places like Governors State. "They could go on interminably," says Hamilton. "Redundant as hell."

Unlike the University of Chicago, which was private, the board of governors overseeing Governors State comprised people appointed by the governor of Illinois. Regina knew it was important that they ask who she was and take her seriously despite her youth. As Bacon remembers the contract negotiation, "She shows up in the biggest red hat I've ever seen. She created drama. That was the actress in her."

Echoing everyone else, Tom Hamilton recalls, "She was infectious in her appearance but so damn confident. She came into a room and had every confidence that she was the smartest, most charismatic person in the room, and had a way of flattering you that was very effective."

But Governors State, like the University of Chicago, stalled the contract negotiations. "They weren't going to give us anything," says Bacon. "And they weren't used to negotiating with civil-service people. The issue dealt with classifications. But the pay of the classifications never kept pace with the economy. So Regina met with the university's Merit Systems Board (a group she was already familiar with from organizing Chicago State) and convinced them to send people to the university to audit every position in the unit. The result was that people eventually got upgrades!"

But not immediately. The university continued to stall. Once again, Regina figured out how to make them come back to the table before the contract was up.

"She organized a strike to occur on the day that 3,000 special needs kids were coming to the campus on busses for the Special Olympics!" remembers Bacon with awe. "Busses that would not be allowed to cross the picket line with handicapped kids inside!"

To avert what would have been extremely damaging publicity, the university settled the contract the next day.

"That was selective pressure," says Bacon, whom Regina had finally talked into becoming a union steward. 'You can't give up now,' she said. 'I need you. I have to have you. Just one more time, Phyllis. Just one year.' She could always talk me into it," sighs Phyllis. "No matter what."

❧ *Johnnie Scott*

███████████████████████████

"*I* heard that they [Tom and Regina] needed some help from another housekeeper in the building," recalls Johnnie Scott, now nearly 80 and, ironically, working for the notoriously low-paying, benefit-lacking, and economy-altering Wal-Mart. "So I went there early one morning. Tom was asleep but Regina outlined everything that she wanted done, which was shopping, chores, and taking care of the house. She took care of the animals. Two cats (one obese and the other with kidney/incontinence problems) and a sickly fat rabbit that had its own room.

"When she asked me about myself, I was embarrassed at first to tell her that I had worked as a maid in a hotel, but she told me never to be ashamed of work. She said there was dignity in all work. I was enrolled at that time at Kennedy King College, and she was so glad that I was going back to school that she scheduled around it and gave me three days a week on my own time. She was one of the most gracious women you would ever want to see."

Today in her little home in Mississippi, Johnnie is surrounded by memories and a few possessions—photographs, cookware, dishes, furniture, dresses, shoes, and hats—that belonged to the woman she came to know briefly and love like a daughter.

"Regina's days started early. She would leave about 7 or 7:30. Sometimes Ray Hamilton would pick her up. Sometimes she would drive. Her evenings were for Tom. Quality time. They'd go for walks. She was a great cook. She entertained two to three times a week: Teamsters, bankers, somebody was coming into town and she would fix for them. Elaborate dishes. Fine china."

On one of those evenings, an intimate party of eight included Tom's coworker Sarah Brown and her husband, Charlie, as well as Ray Hamilton's son Tom and his girlfriend, Maggie.

"I remember Regina making Tom trek to four separate North Side boutique food stores that morning to pick up steaks, vegetables, fish, and bread," recalls Hamilton. "For us! I wouldn't drive 20 miles to four boutique stores if Queen Elizabeth were on the guest list!"

The meal was impressive enough for Hamilton, the son of an Irish Teamster with nine kids to feed, to be astounded by it decades later. "I remember Regina dumping a pound of butter and a half gallon of orange juice into a pot and telling me to 'keep stirring so it doesn't burn.' And I'm stirring and stirring and finally, finally saying, 'We better turn off the heat or there won't be anything left.' To which Regina responded, 'That's the point. We're trying to get to the essence.' And I'm looking at it, thinking, my mom used to ration orange juice like it was WWII in our middle-class family!"

Tom Hamilton's peasant palate still has a salivary memory of the most marbled steaks he had ever seen, salmon soufflé, and liver pâté. He also remembers Charlie Brown's assessment of the meal to be, "My taste buds are having an orgasm."

The aftermath of Regina's epicurean production is as etched in Tom's memory as Shelley Carter's kitchen when the high school–aged Regina baked a cake in it. "A messier kitchen I have never seen," he says. "It looked like she had cooked for the Eighth Army. Pots and pans everywhere; the counters and floors covered with cartons, wrappers, powder, and slop."

The woman who was once embarrassed to admit that she cleaned hotel rooms for a living, however, was happy to clean up after Regina's dinner parties. Johnnie Scott still smiles at the memories of Regina, dressed in Tom's shirts and jeans, cooking his favorite dishes while listening to country western music. "I always knew who was home last by what the radio was set to: US99 [country] or WFMT [classical]." I believe Tom would have been a snob if it hadn't been for Regina. He came to know people through Regina."

In addition to her dinner parties, Regina took great pains to cook meals that Tom would enjoy. "If she was coming home late or not at all, she would cook for Tom a beautiful plate of lamb chops and peas and wrap his dishes before she left, leaving me instructions or telling him to eat it cold."

Because she was gone a lot, Regina used notes that she taped to the refrigerator to communicate with both Tom and Johnnie.

"Every time Tom came to that fridge, he was looking for a note and so was I," recalls Johnnie, trying to smile through the fresh pain of talking about Regina 22 years after her death. "She invented the phrase *no problem* and she did things simply. Tom would beat around the bush but she went right to the core. On several occasions something came up and she said, 'No problem.' She would write Thomas a note 'Johnnie needs this' and he would do it. He was crazy in love with her and it didn't matter what she did or how it was."

Although Tom says that he and Gina argued occasionally about her long hours and late nights, Johnnie never saw any indication of discord. "If they did argue it was probably about money but he'd always give in. The money part didn't bother him. He would say, 'Regina wants it.'

"I remember making up the bed and there was a big crystal vase and me and the cat was playing and it broke. I wrestled with it all day and finally wrote a note to Regina and Tom. Tom didn't say nothing [when he read it], but I could see on his face that he was hurt. But Regina said, 'Well, everything gets broken sometime.' She said, 'Our hearts get broken and this is no better than a heart.' She made it easy for me. It didn't even faze her that this was an expensive piece. She never put a price on anything."

Ironically, Johnnie shared a Valentine's Day birthday with Regina as well as dress and shoe sizes. "She would go to New York and shop for me as well as her. She was just an extraordinary person. She wanted everybody to have the same life she had.

"She was the sort of person who could adapt to any situation. I remember a time when she gave me time off for vacation and Tom forgot to pay me. I lived on Justine on the South Side. At the time, it wasn't a suitable neighborhood. It was bad. And I remember lookin' out the window and here comes Regina walking by herself. Bringing me my paycheck. She wasn't afraid of nobody. 'Have a nice vacation,' she told me, 'its better with pay.' That's the way she phrased it: 'It's better with pay.'"

The woman sure loved her hats…even when they were scarves.

 *Hoffa*

$\mathcal{I}$n May of 1981, Regina was selected to deliver the keynote speech at Local 743's annual Stewards' Seminar, affectionately called Teamster Prom. It was a huge honor. She was only 31 years old and very excited about the prospect of thanking the stewards who she felt were the most important and most put-upon members of the union, and for the opportunity to educate and inspire them. Regina believed that the stewards were the face of the union in the workplace and, as a result, the most important people in the union. She was aware of the problems they faced on a daily basis, appreciated their efforts, and understood their need for renewal and inspiration.

For personal inspiration, she played a record of a speech that her hero Jimmy Hoffa had delivered at a Teamster convention 15 years before. She played it over and over again, listening to Hoffa's elevated ideals as well as his flattened vowels.

The two Teamsters, as it turns out, had a lot in common. Both were born on Valentine's Day. Both came from humble means. Both were committed, charismatic, and brilliant leaders. Both inspired loyal followers as well as bitter jealousies.

Although Regina never met the internationally notorious labor leader whose name is synonymous with the word *Teamster*, she idolized him and found inspiration in his words as much as his accomplishments. On February 14, 1913, James Riddle Hoffa was born in Brazil, Indiana. Raised in the warehouses of Detroit, Michigan, Hoffa dropped out of school at age 14 to help support his widowed mother and siblings. After the stock market crash of 1929, he helped organized his first impromptu strike.

By age 19 Hoffa was a business agent for the local Teamsters union in Detroit. After years as a Detroit local vice-president with a reputation for being tough but fair, Hoffa met a former prizefighter, Paul "Red" Dorfman, who would alter Hoffa's fate incalculably through an introduction to underworld figures who were in turn responsible for winning Chicago mob support. Support that facilitated Hoffa's ascent as Teamster boss.

When Regina Polk was nurturing baby farm animals into health, Hoffa was cultivating an idea of creating what would become one of the most infamous financial dynasties of modern times: the United Brotherhood of Teamsters Central States Pension Fund. Through a combination of resources from Teamster locals in 22 states, the new pension fund would become a vehicle that could provide portable pensions for truck drivers who frequently changed jobs. It would also become a gigantic piggy bank, perhaps the largest unregulated bank in the country. And it would be operated at the disposal of Hoffa and, it has been repeatedly alleged, his friends in the Mafia to whom he owed his position.

In 1956, when new allegations were made that the leadership of the Teamsters Union was involved in illegal financial activities, the Select Committee on Labor (a group that included Joe McCarthy, Barry Goldwater, John F. Kennedy, and Robert Kennedy) decided that the allegations merited investigation. The committee discovered several financial irregularities that led to hearings and eventually the conviction of the International Brotherhood's president, Dave Beck, for using union funds to renovate his home.

At that time, the 44-year-old Hoffa, with backing from friends in obscure places, was elected president of the International Brotherhood of Teamsters Union. His earliest accomplishment was to negotiate the Teamsters' first national contract with trucking companies. By creating industry consolidation into multi-employer negotiating groups, Hoffa was able to create a national master fleet contract that tripled wages and substantially increased benefits. Membership in the International Brotherhood swelled above 2 million.

But Robert Kennedy was not finished with the Teamsters. With the former Teamsters president in prison, Kennedy began investigating Hoffa and eventually charged him with corruption, claiming that Hoffa had misappropriated $9.5 million in union funds and had corruptly done deals with employers. In a lengthy televised interrogation, Kennedy grilled the powerful Teamster leader over his union's ties to organized crime.

Although the jury found Hoffa not guilty, George Meany, then president of the AFL-CIO, did not agree with the verdict and suspended Hoffa and the Teamsters Union from their association. By 1960, when Regina was ten years old, Hoffa was as popular as ever with his members whose lives had improved dramatically under him and he was reelected as president of the Teamsters Union.

That same year, he was a generous benefactor to Richard M. Nixon in his unsuccessful bid for presidency against the brother of Hoffa's enemy Robert Kennedy. Once in office, John Kennedy appointed his brother attorney general, and Robert resumed his investigations into Hoffa's activities—this time charging Hoffa with taking money from the union's pension fund.

President John F. Kennedy was shot and killed in Dallas, Texas, in November of 1963. A few months later, after one mistrial, Hoffa was found guilty of jury tampering and sentenced to eight years in prison.

Before leaving for prison in 1964, Hoffa returned an old favor. He granted Alan Dorfman, the stepson of his old pal Red Dorfman and close associate of Local 743's Don Peters, control of a pot of gold: the infamous Central States Pension Fund.

In December of 1971 President Richard Nixon ordered Hoffa's release one year earlier than his sentence called for but barred him from Teamster activity. (Later, FBI records revealed that Nixon had received illegal campaign donations from the Teamsters Union in exchange for a presidential pardon.)

After his release, Hoffa traveled the country campaigning for prison reform while trying to reclaim his position with the Teamsters. But on July 30, 1975, one year after Regina had begun her career with Local 743, Jimmy Hoffa disappeared on his way to a meeting with a Detroit gangster.

Seven years later, Hoffa was legally declared "presumed dead." Two years after that, in 1984, Alan Dorfman was murdered gangland style in a suburban Chicago parking lot after disregarding the standard mob warning: two bullets in his bumper.

But in 1981 Regina listened to the voice of her idol while she prepared her speech to the stewards. A speech that would be historic as well and she knew it. She, too, was dealing with an environment hostile to union activity. During his first term in office, President Ronald Reagan had:

- slashed the budget of the National Labor Relations Board, making it nearly impossible for agents to carry out investigations or issue unfair labor practice complaints
- filled the NLRB with pro-management members
- fired 13,000 striking federal air traffic controllers
- allowed (encouraged) the air traffic controllers' employers to replace them
- had five union leaders prosecuted for striking against the government
- outlawed the air traffic controllers union entirely

Unions were in a state of disgrace. And union busting had become the newest growth industry in America. With each session of Congress, new bills were introduced to further restrict unions from organizing and representing their members.

At that time, Local 743, with more than 30,000 members, was the largest Teamster local in the country. The "man-age-ment" of unions was guarded by men of a certain age who meant to keep control. But they were struggling.

A woman had never before had the opportunity to be as influential or unforgettable as Regina would be in her speech to the stewards. She had long since proven her value, her passion, and her ability. There wasn't a doubt in anyone's mind as to who would lead them next.

Bastards with Briefcases: Protection of Your Contractual Gains

By Regina Polk

INTERNATIONAL BROTHERHOOD OF
TEAMSTERS
Chauffeurs, Warehousemen & Helpers of America
Warehouse, Mail Order, Office, Technical and
Professional Employees Union

Local 743 Stewards' Seminar
May 9, 1981

*M*any of you have been in the Teamsters' organization long enough to have known or perhaps met one of the truly great union leaders of our time—James Hoffa. It is perhaps the great regret of my life that I was too young to have met the man and to have fully understood what contributions he made to the union movement. I guess about the time he left office, my one great concern was trying to graduate from high school.

I was fortunate enough to hear a taped speech that he made in Detroit in 1966. One thing in particular that he said in that speech has been very much on my mind the last year or so as I look around at the challenges that face organized labor.

In that speech and many times before, he reminded us that the Teamsters have many enemies—and that those enemies are the people who would take away from us what we have built, what we have gained for our members. He said that if we are going to survive, it is our burden as Teamsters and trade unionists to have to continually fight for that survival. He said that we can never assume that the contracts we've built, the gains we've made, the security of the organization are safe—that there will always be those who would, if we let them, strip us of all those achievements.

It seems to me that what he said then has never been more relevant than right now.

It is not news to you that there is a tremendous wave of anti-unionism sweeping this country now. You can't pick up a paper or a journal without reading that labor is too big—corrupt, lazy, unresponsive to its members—and that labor is some pathetic dinosaur whose time has come and gone. We hear one pronouncement after another which happily predicts the decline and collapse of the American labor movement.

The National Labor Relations Board, which was set up in the 1930s under a national policy of peaceful and cooperative labor-management relations, that was established to encourage workers to organize and bargain collectively with their employer, now spends much of its time and OUR tax dollars processing movements to oust unions.

Each session of Congress, bills are introduced which would further restrict our ability to organize and represent our members.

In the Illinois Senate several weeks ago, an event occurred which shocked all of the Illinois labor movement—a "right to work" bill in Illinois was voted out of committee.

But perhaps the most disgusting outgrowth of this anti-unionism is a new breed of union. They don't come with brass knuckles or clubs any more to beat unionism out of us; instead, they come in their three-piece suits, armed with briefcases, charts and graphs—and they come to tell the working men and women of America of the EVILS OF UNIONIZATION. They twist and distort and lie—and by the time they are through, the word which has meant everything to millions of people in this country has become a dirty word: UNIONS. They perpetrate what is truly the BIG LIE—that to join a union is not just a fruitless venture—but by joining a union, one will bring disaster to both himself and his employer.

Right now there are approximately 150,000 law firms and consulting firms in this nation whose primary purpose is to bust unions, and the number grows weekly—and why not? The wages are great. These professional union busters have created the fastest-growing, the most profitable industry on the scene today, and that industry is currently raking in about $500 million a year for their services. Employers are happy to pay these professionals up to $5,000 a week to keep their companies non-union.

At first, these professionals concentrated their efforts on keeping unions out of companies. But increasingly they bring their message of "Let us make you union-free" to those employers who have had union contracts for years. And that is exactly how they sell their product: "A Union-Free Environment"—and if that sounds like an exterminating service, that is exactly what it is. Their success rate at these exterminations of unions is alarming—they have beaten unions in approximately 85 percent of the elections in which they participated.

And if that message has escaped anyone—let me make it clear. They intend to exterminate us—they exist for no other purpose—they intend to drive organized labor out of existence. This is not a collection of isolated incidents—IT IS NOTHING SHORT OF A MASSIVE ASSAULT ON EVERYTHING WE BELIEVE IN.

If any one of you believes that this could never happen to you—that the union has been in your company too long, that you've worked too hard, that your contract is too strong, that the company has gotten used to your presence—DON'T KID YOURSELF.

YOUR COMPANY DOESN'T WANT A UNION ANY MORE

NOW THAN THEY DID WHEN THEY FOUGHT YOU THE FIRST TIME THE UNION SHOWED UP. They fought you then, they've fought you ever since, and they'll continue to fight you.

You know that your company, if they thought it would work, would pay almost anything to wake up one morning and find the union gone, the contract gone, and YOU GONE—so that they would once again have a free hand.

And if you still doubt that these exterminators could take your union—I wish I had time here to read a list of the names of your company representatives who have attended those slimy $500 a day "How to Beat the Union" seminars. They don't go to those seminars because they don't know how else to spend $500. THEY GO SO THEY CAN LEARN HOW TO BUST YOUR UNION. Employers have caught the smell of blood—and there are now professional exterminators available who will fulfill their dreams of once again being non-union.

And worst of all is that this dirty, filthy business of busting unions—of draining the lifeblood from workers in this country, of taking bread from the mouths of working families—is being presented to workers in a clean, neat, beautiful little package, that reeks of Madison Avenue advertising. It hardly seems possible, but it is being presented in a form that is distracting workers from their own real needs and interests in alarming numbers.

And if we're waiting around for someone else to pull the plug on these bastards with the briefcases—then we're sounding our own death knell. It's us—us, not the politicians, not the government, but us alone who will expose this outrageous deception that is being perpetrated against working people.

We must expose this plague on the land for what it is—an all-out attempt to strip us of everything that we've worked to build and protect and to send us back to the sweatshops from which we came.

And how do we confront such a vicious and sophisticated enemy? To do so is no easy task. But we have at our disposal the best possible weapon: THE TRUTH AND FACTS ABOUT ORGANIZED LABOR.

It is a message that has gone unsung for too long, and I blame our-selves, our organizations, and our leaders for not repeating and repeating this message to our members and to the public about us—what it is we do and what we have devoted our lives to—for it is our best offensive tactic.

And that message embodies what brought trade unionism into existence in the first place and what brought YOU into what is the most thankless and difficult job that exists—that of being a Union Steward.

You have taken the responsibility of protecting the principles of unionism—of protecting your contract and your fellow workers. WHY? For the money? There is precious little of that. For the glory? I haven't seen any.

You took the job because you believe in the dignity of work and those who earn their living by it.

You believe that every person who works should come to work and bow their head to no one.

You believe in the right of workers to make decisions about those things that affect their lives.

You believe that every person is entitled to the best price for their toil.

You believe in the dignity and respect and rights that come only from a written contract.

And, most of all, you believe it is your duty to protect all those things.

The message to our members and to the public should go on to say that unions are as needed today as ever. This idea that since we've won the eight-hour day we're no longer needed is bullshit.

As long as there are employers who would make their profits off our backs—unions are needed.

As long as there is discrimination against ANYONE—unions are needed.

As long as women workers make 59 cents for every dollar that men make—unions are needed.

And most importantly, we must remind our members again and again that YOUR COMPANY NEVER HANDED YOU A DAMN THING—that every right you enjoy, every wage increase you are guaranteed, every benefit you're entitled to was fought for—and won—by YOU.

We must remind them that while the campaign of vilification of the Teamsters Union rages on and on in the press, we are still the largest and strongest union in the world; we still engage in and win more elections than any other union; when another union needs help they come to us; and while our brother and sister unions are shrinking, we continue to grow.

And to our critics in the press—who know nothing of what it is to labor for a living or what we are truly all about—we say this:

WHAT NEWSPAPER EDITOR, TV ANCHORMAN, OR JOUR-NALIST HAS EVER BROUGHT YOU ONE SINGLE CLAUSE OF YOUR CONTRACT—you, by your own blood, sweat, and toil—you won that contract.

And that, too, was first said by James Hoffa.

We cannot afford to assume that even our members know these truths and these facts—not to mention the public. Those members who came to us after the initial struggle was won DO NOT KNOW WHAT THE UNION HAS ACHIEVED FOR THEM.

IT SIMPLY MUST BE THE TASK OF EACH AND EVERY STEWARD TO GO TO THOSE NEW EMPLOYEES AND TELL THEM WHAT THE UNION IS, WHY IT EXISTS, AND WHY IT MUST ALWAYS CONTINUE TO EXIST.

The steward who ignores this task is the one who will wake up one morning to find these workers who never knew what was accomplished by the union have fallen victim to the man in the three-piece suit, with the charts and graphs.

We must constantly defend and protect the things we've won—and not just at contract time. We must always guard against the erosion of our contracts, for no matter how many shortcomings you may think of your contract having, it is the most precious thing that exists for us in the workplace—it is irreplaceable.

If the steward is too busy, too tired, or too lazy to file that grievance when the contract is violated or someone's rights are abridged—THAT STEWARD SHOULD BE THROWN OUT. For if management sees that you—the face of the union in the plant or office—don't care about the contract, that is the first sign that the union buster could do his dirty business.

If management sees that we are careless, ill prepared, or indifferent to our members, that, too, is a signal to call in the exterminators.

It is your primary job to be constantly on guard for those who would take from us the only thing that gives our work meaning and dignity—the right to speak freely, the right to challenge, and the right to participate. And when there is no union, there are no rights. There is only silence.

There are many of you whom I have had the personal pleasure of sharing difficult times with—either during your organizing effort, during negotiations, or on a picket line. And I know personally you've paid your dues in a very special way. There are several brothers here in this audience who have just recently had to stand the test of fire—and they deserve our recognition.

They work for a company that has been represented by Local 743 for almost 30 years—that means something to me because it is my whole lifetime. Their company is known nationwide as one of the great union busters in the country. But, after 30 years of good representation, of good contracts, and of hard, thankless work by these men—the workers in that company suddenly found themselves being challenged by the company to fight once again for the very survival of their union—to do again what they had done nearly 30 years ago. The labor board set up an election and that began the most brutal, vicious, anti-union campaign I ever hope to be involved in. They pounded those employees for weeks with meeting after meeting, they pumped out 27 pieces of literature containing the most vicious and destructive lies that could be manufactured about their union—and they threatened and threatened and threatened. And when the workers went home to enjoy a union-won holiday, the company called them at home and threatened them more—until we thought that not even the strongest among that group would withstand this kind of incredible pressure.

But when the voting was ended, and the last ballot was counted, these workers, by a vote of four to one, told their company once again after 30 years that the plant WAS NOT GOING TO BE UNION FREE.

[At this point in her speech, Regina introduces the election committee: Perry Rogers, Cliff Phillips, Albert Alexander, and Ernest Dubois.]

The lesson that we all must learn from their experience and their courage is an urgent one. We must conduct ourselves always with the knowledge that at any give time—we must be able to meet the challenge—and we must return to our offices and our plants with renewed vigor, not just with a view toward what we must gain in the future, but with a constant view of what we must protect.

AND IF WE DO OUR JOBS, we will not only survive this period of anti-unionism—we will grow stronger and larger.

In fact, as the weeks wear on, our importance to workers increases steadily—for when the laws that have been passed to give protections to workers in this nation have been repealed and gutted as they are each day of this administration, when OSHA has been rendered hollow and meaningless, and when Title VII of the Civil Rights Act is lying wounded and helpless, there will be only one place for workers to find safety, security, and protection—the same place they have always found it, WITH US.

* * *

At the end of Regina's speech, the 31-year-old Teamster received a standing ovation of recognition and appreciation. Then, typical of Regina, instead of basking in her own glory, she generously handed off recognition to others.

"She introduced three guys in the audience who had been stewards longer than I have been alive," says Melva Hunter with awe. "People were once again on their feet applauding, recognizing those guys for the importance of what they did, understanding what it took."

There was no one in that room who didn't recognize the power of Regina Polk.

 *Grievances*

*W*hen a grievance is presented by an employee, it is the job of the union steward to file a charge for that person in accordance to the grievance procedure written into each individual contract. Although the procedures may differ from one contract to another, the basic outline is this:

> At the first stage a steward files the grievance and arranges a meeting between the steward, the grievant (the injured party), and a supervisor, usually at the departmental level. If the parties fail to resolve their differences at this stage they proceed to either a second or third stage (depending on how large the department is and how many bureaucratic layers it contains), with the final step being a meeting between the labor relations representative from human resources and, usually, the business agent from the union, although in some cases the steward will do this. Finally, if the dispute is still unresolved, the matter goes to binding arbitration. Not

all contracts provide for this, but it is a sign of a strong contract if it includes binding arbitration because it means a neutral third party settles unresolved disputes. The arbitrator comes from the Federal Mediation and Arbitration Service and is chosen by a complicated joint process laid out in the contract.

It's expensive to take a grievance to arbitration and a lot of unions never do it. But in the first two to three years of the University of Chicago contract, Regina took many, many grievances to arbitration. This was a costly but smart strategy showing 743's willingness to pursue these cases to the end and reinforcing the seriousness of the union's commitment to enforcing the contract. According to University of Chicago union steward Gary Mamlin, "Regina constantly emphasized the importance of enforcing the contract. The need to be constantly vigilant with respect to the contract. She was aware of the fact that one of the most demoralizing things to union members is that they get a contract and then they see that it's not enforced."

Many times a lawyer is hired to argue the grievance (one of the reasons grievance arbitration is so expensive), and Local 743 had a law firm to represent them in grievances. Regina, however, was able to handle even complicated arbitration cases on her own.

"She was an advocate for people who had no power by themselves," says Melva Hunter. "She was frequently their only recourse. But she worked for the workers, knowing that their jobs depended on what she did or didn't do."

"Whenever Gina wore a hat," remembers Edna Hunter, "we'd say, 'she has an arbitration today.'"

"She became very, very good at handling grievances," recalls Robert W. McAllister, an arbitrator with 40 years of experience. "She was diligent and overly protective of her members—more so than any union representative that I've ever come across. She took it personally. She spent the time. And I had a profound respect for her."

"Hamilton would go into grievances unprepared and win," says Ray Kujawa. "He flew by the seat of his pants but was very bright. So while other business agents would bring in a lawyer, Hamilton, like Regina, could do it himself. They were a formidable duo—brains and brawn."

Gary Mamlin first met Regina when he was working in the university bookstore and challenged some of the administration's abuses in terms of supply requisitions for expensive and questionable items. "I called 'the pretty lady from the union,' as she was known around here. She came in and was very protective. She dressed fashionably, really smart. She was animated and intense. She had a strong personality and expressed herself in an impassioned way, telling the administrators that I was only trying to do the right thing and said that if they so much as look at me the wrong way, she'll tie them up in so many arbitrations they won't know what to do next."

When the university employees got their new contract, Mamlin realized that the bookstore was not following that contract in terms of how they were filling positions, so he called Regina again. "We went over the contract, addressed the issues, and she talked me into becoming a union steward. Much more than a pretty lady, when we went into grievance meetings, she was serious. It was no party. She was enthusiastic and had wonderful rhetorical skills and analytical skills. She never hesitated to adopt a confrontational style when needed, feeling that it was an appropriate reaction to the employer's confrontational way of dealing with its employees. She defended ferociously her members when managers attempted to abuse them, believing that the unions should do more than just guarantee a wage, that it should also see to it that its members were treated respectfully."

University of Chicago union steward Edna Hunter remembers Regina's strategy in grievances with admiration. "When we went in for a grievance she would allow the supervisor or administrator to set the tone of the meeting. She would make a statement about why we were there and then that person was allowed to talk. And based on how that person responded, that's the way the meeting would go. If the person was a diplomat and stuck with what was in the grievance, it was okay. If for any reason they challenged her authority, she would immediately change. She would take control and let them know it in no uncertain terms that she was in control. It was almost as though when these guys looked at her, they thought, *Oh, she's a pushover,* and man she would quote sections of the contract and half of them didn't even know what the contract said! She was awesome. Flying solo! She really impressed us. If she were living today, she would be setting policy and making decisions about things on a national level."

"Once we got our contract," says University of Chicago union steward Maggie Newman, "I got to know her in the realm of grievance meetings. Arbitrations. We had a good cop–bad cop routine down. She would go in there and screech and scream, stamp her feet, and get red in the face. It was all a big act. I would be the voice of cool reason. I would say, 'I can't control her much longer, hurry up and give us what we want.' And it was very effective a lot of the time."

After a grievance meeting, the two would go out for hot fudge sundaes. Once Regina told Maggie, "I'm the only person I know whose job description requires tantrums. It's so great because I get all my aggression out."

Well, maybe not all her aggressions. After losing an election to organize St. Joseph's Hospital in Joliet, Illinois, Regina and both Hamiltons went into the local bar for a drink. Before long they were approached by a couple of consultant union busters (bastards with briefcases) who were coming in to celebrate their victory and made the mistake of approaching Regina in a "nothing-personal-let's-have-a-drink" way. Regina took it personally.

"She took her drink and threw it in this guy's face," says Tom Hamilton, who was barely out of his teens at the time. "These were 45-year-old white guys in business suits! She knew those guys weren't going to punch her out—but if they had tried, they would have been laying there dead. My father admired her combativeness.

Still, the mouth, the temper, you couldn't get away with it if you weren't a good-looking white girl. I don't know if she had a temper— she thought things through more than that—but she certainly affected one à la Hoffa."

Despite the theatrics and her battles with Robert Simpson, Hamilton frequently saw a softer side of Regina. "She really did care about the people who counted on her. Many a time she would come to me when members had told her something and she would say, 'Robert, that's not right, they can't do these poor women or these poor people like that.'"

The Team-star at Local 743.

Victory! Don Peters and his team celebrate University of Chicago results.

Open for business. Regina Polk made her self available to discuss union matters with workers by planting herself in visible locations at the University of Chicago and other workplaces.

Humanities 101

A case that demonstrates Regina's "do whatever it takes" vision as well as hands-on commitment involved a University of Chicago secretary who had been raped and robbed in her home on a Saturday night.

The Monday after the incident, the worker (Katherine Karvunis) reported to her newly transferred position with (ironically) the social sciences collegiate division of the U of C. But during the week that followed, Karvunis was unable to sleep and developed what she called a "growing sense of disorganization." By the next week, she said she felt "totally helpless" and walked out of her office. When a coworker asked her where she was going, she responded, "I quit."

Three days after leaving her job, Karvunis realized the significance of what she had done, contacted the personnel office and her supervisor, and explained that she would like to return to work. She was told that that would be impossible. So she called Regina and Regina called Jonathan Z. Smith, the assistant dean of the college, who said, "I just don't want her back."

Because Karvunis had resigned voluntarily, Regina couldn't file a grievance, so she took the story to the student newspaper. The *Chicago Maroon* ran the story, and the embarrassed university reinstated the secretary.

The original terms of reinstatement considered Karvunis a "new hire," however, meaning that she would lose her seniority and face a 90-day probationary period, during which time she would work without union protection. Karvunis reported for work as instructed but was then asked to sign a statement verifying that, although she had suffered an unfortunate experience, the university was in no way responsible and, therefore, owed her nothing. When Regina heard about it, she exploded. Calling the statement an "insulting travesty," she immediately filed notice of intent to pursue the grievance to the next step.

In a subsequent meeting with Karvunis, Regina was angered by Smith's insistence on discussing the technicalities of how a grievance is organized and filed and the assertion that the issues involved were not part of the union contract.

"When the contract is silent," Regina said, "basic human dignity prevails."

Smith was intractable and told Regina that their humanitarian feelings only extend as far as giving Karvunis her job back as a new hire. He then issued a written response to the grievance, stating that because the worker "voluntarily resigned" from her position, she was not entitled to union benefits. The statement also mentioned that she was reinstated as a new hire for "humanitarian reasons."

Regina then arranged another meeting—this one including Edward Coleman, the director of personnel, as well as Sherry Fischer, the University Medical Center chaplain intern. At that meeting the intern, who worked with Karvunis, explained that her behavior was understandable and almost predictable after her trauma. "There is a definite rape trauma syndrome," Fischer reported, "involving a period of disorganization that lasts about two or three days. This is followed by a longer period of reorganization. The victim is displaying the usual attempt at reorganizing her life after a crisis. A rape is a major crisis, in which the victim can feel grief, just as though she has lost a loved one."

Vindicated and still unhappy with the university's position, Regina told The *Chicago Maroon* reporter that "the union wants the story made public because we want the university community to see how a distinguished faculty member and administrator, who represents an institution devoted to humanitarian causes and liberal ideas, put his theories into practice."

Smith, the newspaper reported, was unavailable for comment.

♥ *Loss*

███████████████████████████████

A few weeks before Christmas of 1982, Aldens, Inc., a $300-million-a-year catalog house on Chicago's West Side, closed. Two thousand six hundred union members—mostly women—were let go. Unfortunately, they didn't have anywhere to go nor any skills to take with them.

"Aldens was an incredible place in terms of being 80 percent minority and 85 percent female," says Melva Hunter. "Most of the people who had been laid off had worked at Aldens most of their lives."

"So many people had lost their jobs," recalls Aldens worker Sirlena Perry. "The line was so long at the unemployment office, you had to arrive an hour before the office opened to get served that day."

Regina took their tragedy to heart. She'd seen plant closings and the terrible human toll it takes before at other catalog houses including Spiegel's where, according to her housekeeper, "Regina was so distraught that those people didn't have any money and some of them were depending on paychecks that day that she wrote them checks out of her account to give them money for the weekend. She would do stuff like that."

When Montgomery Ward closed its plant at Chicago Avenue and Halsted Street earlier that year, hundreds of workers, many of them non-English-speaking, stood outside in confusion and despair. Regina was beside herself.

"Some mornings early when we would meet," Ray Hamilton reported later, "Regina would come without makeup and I would know that something difficult had happened. She hurt with people and worried about them particularly in layoff situations. The pain she felt for those people was as deep as they felt for themselves. She would frequently talk about the potential of child beating and wife beating, divorce and separation, and she would truly cry and hurt, and I'd give her a couple of old bullshit stories about the Irish or something and it would straighten her out. She could put on her makeup and go out and fight with the rest of the people."

At the Governors State Christmas party in 1982, all Regina could think about were the recently laid off Aldens workers. "She was so sad," says former union steward Phyllis Bacon. "She told me the people at Aldens were being laid off and she said that they had nothing. They had folded cardboard boxes for their whole lives and some of them couldn't even read the pink slip. The next day, after they closed the warehouse, some of the members stood on the corner because they didn't know what to do with themselves. And then it was Regina to the rescue."

By then, Christmas of 1982, the 32-year-old Teamster's stardom as an organizer, a negotiator, and a business agent was well established. Despite Teamster scandal on a national level, she had worked tirelessly to remedy inequalities and injustice through the organization of workers, broadened the union's horizons through the massive influx of women she recruited into its ranks, and created little pockets of hope. In short, she had power. So when she went to Don Peters on behalf of the displaced workers at Aldens, he agreed that the Teamsters had to do something to help those people. After all, they had paid their dues.

With Peters's support, Regina began to organize her team.

"We met in a restaurant," recalls Melva Hunter, who had experienced a plant layoff herself four years before. "She was coming in from a picket line and looked lovely. Slacks, small heels, shirt collar turned up."

In the four years since her own layoff, Hunter had been working for the state of Illinois on plant closings and knew all about Aldens.

When Regina said to Melva, "You have to come help me with the Aldens workers," she was probably not surprised that Melva didn't turn her down. The surprise may have been the close bond that would develop between the beautifully dressed young business agent and the former factory worker who became one of her best friends.

Echoing the sentiment of so many women, Hunter recalls, "I don't know where I would be without her. She taught me how to dress and how to function. Regina had two books about Hoffa and she wanted me to love them as she did."

In addition to Melva Hunter, the Illinois State AFL-CIO Manpower Assistance Program brought other resource persons to Local 743's headquarters. To inform the jobless workers about what they were entitled to and guide them to the various agencies involved in helping the unemployed, the team created workshops all over Chicago—in churches, in union halls, or anyplace else Regina could find. And at those workshops Regina talked to the workers and listened to them.

"The women loved her," Hunter recalls. "She was incredible. She used to say, 'Labor leaders and bosses are one thing, but if you can ever get at the guy with the baseball cap or woman answering the phone, you can get almost anything done."

Many of the workers lacked the basic math and writing skills to get into training programs. "So Regina went to city colleges and found a teacher to help the displaced workers brush up on basic skills in order to pass entrance exams," says Hunter.

Soon after, she began job clubs or programs to teach the displaced workers new skills, including basics like reading, writing, math, typing, résumé writing, and how to dress for an interview. Later still, she expanded the workshops to focus on handling stress, job-seeking skills, remedial reading, and on-the-job training.

"We told them that change is opportunity," says Hunter. "We were not dewy-eyed social workers. We told them that they can make it together. We introduced them to job clubs and hundreds of them joined."

Sirlena Perry joined. After receiving a letter from Local 743 about the training, she enrolled in a nine-month program to brush up on English grammar, improve typing skills, and learn interviewing techniques including how to dress. The program gave Perry the skills she needed to get back into the workforce. "The job I have now and have held for over 20 years is due to the retraining program."

Around that time, Regina discovered to her great joy that she was pregnant. Tom's response was physical: he laid back and put a pillow on his face. "I had no idea what was he thinking," Regina said to her friends.

Tom remembers that he and Regina had disagreed over the idea. She wanted a baby. He didn't feel ready. "I had recently taken a job at Exchange National Bank as executive vice-president," he says, "and Regina was working all the time."

But the couple quickly embraced the idea, even though Regina continued to work long hours. "Regina was such an angel," recalls Hunter. "I knew her feet were hurting because she kept taking off her shoes while speaking to the women. After working all day long," says Hunter, "Regina would stay at night to work the job clubs—even after we had hired someone else to do stress counseling."

Still, Regina felt that what the union was doing wasn't enough. She knew that she needed more than borrowed space and limited supplies. Her vision was to buy deserted Chicago storefronts that had closed and establish professional training centers in them; she spent every free second looking for sources of potential funding.

She quickly became so well versed on the legislation and worker rights that the Illinois AFL-CIO asked her to conduct workshops throughout the state for other laid-off workers. Through early pregnancy, she worked tirelessly with her friend Melva Hunter to coordinate the programs and willingly went anywhere to help displaced workers. She also got others involved, including politicians like Governor James R. Thompson, who was concerned politically about all the job losses.

Yet, after all Regina was doing and had done, according to Melva, she was still underestimated by her own brotherhood until the press started writing about her. Only then was she invited to speak at the union's executive board meeting about trying to find funding for the displaced workers.

Regina was anything but bitter about her lack of celebrity within the union. Upon receiving the invitation, Hunter recalls her saying, "Oh, my God, I'm so happy."

In March of 1983, Regina miscarried. She and Tom were devastated.

"When they first lost the baby and she was coming home," remembers her housekeeper Johnnie, "we just ran into the baby's room and Tom was throwing all the baby clothes out, packing so she would have nothing to remind her. I'd never seen him like that. He just didn't want her to be hurt."

"Even after Regina lost the baby," Hunter recalls, "she was still worried about these stupid workshops. About other women who had lost their livelihoods."

Despite her personal sorrow, Regina returned to work quickly. A big piece of her heart was still breaking on the grimy streets of Chicago and in the unemployment lines with the women who needed her. Although she would never know it, her mission would be a success. The displaced Aldens workers would become the first in Chicago to benefit from the Reagan administration's Federal Job Training Partnership Act.

Disillusionment

$\mathcal{A}$ll told, 1983 was a devastating year for the International Brotherhood of Teamsters. The National Labor Relations Board, established in the '30s to encourage workers to organize and bargain collectively with their employers, had been reduced to processing petitions to oust unions. Economic and physical safety, not to mention workers' rights and human dignity, seemed like a thing of the past.

Air traffic controllers were inexperienced. Savings and loans were closing at an alarming rate. Bankruptcies were daily occurrences. And industry, the backbone of America's economy, was shutting its doors in the faces of workers, many of whom were too poorly educated to read the pink slips with which they had been presented and were returning day after day to stand in the cold and wonder what was going on.

The last thing that organized labor needed was a scandal, but that's just what they got. In order to circumvent government legislation aimed at dismantling union solidarity, top Teamster management in International had been—once again—engaging in risky business with dubious individuals that had been their "friends" for decades. And they got caught.

While poor and unskilled workers were literally left standing in the cold, Teamsters president Roy L. Williams and four others were standing in the heat of federal court. They were convicted on 11 counts of conspiracy, fraud, and interstate commerce in a case concerning a bribe to Senator Howard W. Cannon, a Democrat from Nevada.

Their crime? Conspiring to offer a senator from Nevada a piece of Teamsters-owned land at a bargain price of $200,000—less than what was being offered other bidders—if he would help kill a proposed trucking deregulation bill that would be devastating to their members.

Williams's co-conspirators included Joseph "Joey the Clown" Lombardo, a reputed mob hit man and organized crime's link with labor; Teamsters pension fund trustee Thomas O'Malley; former trustee Andrew "Amos" Massa; and insurance broker Alan Dorfman, who would be brutally murdered in a hotel parking lot while the convictions were being appealed.

Yet, for all the criminal circuses surrounding the Teamsters, no bribe was actually taken. The trucking deregulation legislation bill was passed. And the senator was not indicted. But in the sleight of hand known as appearance versus reality longtime rumors of Teamsters corruption became sealed as reputation. The campaign to vilify unions had won a major battle. And labor leaders lost their position of public trust and, with it, their power.

Still, a battle is not a war. And even public image problems as grave as those facing the Teamsters could not eclipse the commitment, care, and hard work being done by labor legends like Regina Polk. Although organized labor's reputation for violence, corruption, and ties to organized crime had reached a new nadir in 1983, there were many who still hoped that this bright, beautiful 33-year-old woman would change things. Reform the corruption. Salvage the ideals and rights being eroded in the lust for profit and management perks that characterized business in the '80s.

As a low seniority business agent, Regina worked harder than ever for a small salary because representing the members well meant everything to her. Yet, when she looked around, she couldn't help but notice that many of the people in her brotherhood were not as committed to enforcing their hard-won contracts. She reportedly saw some of her fellow business agents as paternalistic opportunists or simply incompetents who weren't as responsive to the members as they should be. So despite her round-the-clock schedule and recent miscarriage, she continued handling grievances, often calling on Ray Hamilton and Joel D'Alba for help.

"She could do two jobs," says Gary Mamlin, "but not three. She was tired and started to look it and show it."

After years of defending Peters (sometimes stridently) about his alleged ties to the mob, she began to criticize him—and Bob Simpson as well—for not being more responsive to member grievances.

"She had talked to me about leaving 743 and starting a local and affiliating with another international because Teamsters has a bad reputation in a lot of ways," says her friend Maggie Newman. "She liked the tough guy thing, but at the same time there were some unsavory things in the Teamsters past and she told me that she had seriously considered the idea of taking the University of Chicago and defecting, starting her own independent—or possibly affiliating with the Service Employees International Union, which represents a lot of clerical workers."

Paul Booth remembers listening to Regina's complaints at the time. "I was in a position to give her feedback on what she was encountering, but I don't want to overstate the amount or significance. Regina was quite sharp about figuring stuff out herself. But the life of that local at that time, the way it was then, it had a bunch of workers that were disinclined to meet higher expectations. The goals were modest and so the test was thrown back on the workers. What are you going to make of your opportunity as opposed to what are we going to lead you toward. So what she was encountering in day-to-day life inside that union were obstacles, sources of discontent. What should have been a real engine for the workers that Gina had organized, underperformed. So that's the kind of thing we would talk about. But mostly, I was just a fan. Someone so impressed with her accomplishments. To this day I am pretty awed by what she was able to do."

In the meantime, criticism of her brotherhood did not sit well with Regina's superiors. Don Peters knew she had achieved spectacular popular support. He had made her a business agent after she received an 87 percent strike authorization from the University of Chicago members because the numbers were telling him that she had power.

Tom Heagy remembers it differently. Recalling her frustration and fatigue, he says simply, "Idle musings never became a plan. Gina was very loyal to the Teamsters and moving her members was never a realistic option."

⬤ Air Illinois

*T*uesday, October 12, 1983.

Regina was on a mission. Governor James Thompson had appointed the then 33-year-old Teamster to the Illinois Jobs Coordination Council. She needed money to expand her plans for retraining displaced workers and was on her way to a meeting to further that goal.

Before boarding Air Illinois flight 710 bound for Carbondale, Illinois, Regina made one last call from a public phone at Chicago's Meigs Field. That morning she and Local 743 attorney Joel D'Alba argued a grievance for a middle-aged single woman who worked at a bookstore. Regina, feeling that the woman was entitled to a job upgrade, had spent the time and argued the case. She wanted to make sure there wouldn't be a problem in her absence.

It wasn't the kind of case that most union employees would have fought for let alone followed up on. But according to D'Alba, "All the cases she took up were major to her. Not necessarily high profile but everybody was important to her."

Her friend and coworker Illinois State AFL-CIO representative Melva Hunter did not accompany her as planned because there were thunderstorms in the area and she was afraid of flying in bad weather. "She took my paisley umbrella," Hunter says.

But if Regina thought about the dangers of flying into a thunderstorm at night on a small twin-engine commuter plane, it would have been an uncharacteristic worry. This was a woman who had shown no fear on picket lines or in police lockups, boardrooms or barrooms. No matter what her personal joys or sorrows, "Don't worry about me, I'll be fine," was her often-repeated if inaccurate mantra.

On the plane that night were three crew members and seven passengers, including a mother and a child. In Springfield, Illinois, where the plane stopped briefly, the pilot informed the control tower of a possible electrical problem. But instead of having the plane serviced in Springfield, the pilot asked for and received a lower altitude to fly in. The air traffic controllers probably thought nothing of it.

The last contact with the plane was reported at 8:58 P.M., when the pilots reported they were safely nearing Centralia. Although the pilot made no mention of weather conditions, thunderstorms were reported in the general area, and at 9:05 P.M. the craft disappeared from radar screens.

Ten minutes later, the British Aerospace Hawker Siddeley 748 crashed in rural southern Illinois, 25 miles north of its destination. Impact was just below the top of a ridge. Plane parts and bodies scattered like pieces of confetti over three quarters of a mile of woodland. One of the bodies hit two house trailers on a 40-acre farm. The farmer reported hearing a plane circle above his property, then a loud noise, and then nothing. Light rain. Lightning.

Investigators from the National Transportation Safety Board in Washington were dispatched to the site. Air Illinois had made the final payment on the ten-year-old plane just nine hours earlier.

There were no survivors among the three crew members and seven passengers.

 *Disbelief*

"*W*hen the gates of heaven swung open that night," says Melva Hunter, "and someone asked, 'Who is that beautiful young woman?' I hope they said, 'Her? She's a Teamster.'"

Funeral services were held on a beautiful autumn day at the First Unitarian Church in Hyde Park. Mourners included her husband, Tom, bereft and in shock; fellow Teamsters; management of the companies she had organized; employees of the The Exchange Bank; family members; and friends. The church was packed with people only half willing to believe what had happened. People with puffy faces and red eyes who felt that she was so much larger than life that surely she had survived the crash and this was all a mistake. People who began to search for answers through magical thinking ("She was called to heaven to be with her baby" or "She is now my/our guardian angel").

Her friend and mentor Ray Hamilton delivered the following eulogy:

> When we speak of Regina, we are speaking of happi-
> ness—what she wanted was for people to be happy.
> Regina Polk was a child to me—a gift placed in my life

for whatever reason. A miracle. I have no idea why I was chosen, but was, and every day I thank the giver and the gift. Regina Polk was a fighter. She struggled for the rights of unorganized workers to join a union. She championed the rights of union members to get the best contract possible and then to make sure they received the benefits of their contracts. In a speech Regina gave on May 9, 1981, she said, "We must constantly defend and protect the things that we have won—and not just at contract time. We must always guard against the erosion of our contracts, for no matter how many shortcomings you think your contracts have, it is the most precious thing that exists for us in the workplace." In life as we remember her, Regina was a realist who saw the necessity of big labor as a counterbalance to big business. She lived as she believed and felt that it was more important to actually help one person than to talk about saving the world. Her entire career was with the International Brotherhood of Teamsters Local 743. She was proud to be a Teamster, proud of the union's accomplishments, and constantly worked to make it better. I feel that she died in the line of duty. She was on her way to a meeting that would give dislocated workers better access to job training. She had of late been to many such meetings but always was willing to go the entire mile if it would help her members. This eulogy would not be complete without mentioning Regina's devotion to animals, cooking, hats, shoes, trips to Elizabeth Arden, her family, and her friends. Above all, she was a devoted and wonderful wife. But most of all, she would want each of us to remember her as she was, a woman who cared. I would like to thank Regina's good husband, Thomas, for the opportunity to read his eulogy to Regina; and even more grateful that he has asked me to add some words of my own.

Regina and I spoke of this day many times and obviously because of our age difference we expected the roles to be reversed and that always bothered her greatly.

First, to you, Thomas. Regina loved you very deeply and admired you even more. Her admiration was constantly being shown as she would open her sentences or comments with "Thomas says" or "Thomas said" or "Thomas thinks."

And to her mom and dad; her dear sister, Eileen; her brother-in-law, Stan; her nephew, Mike—while you were separated by many miles, she loved each of you very much. She spoke of you very often and you were always in her thoughts. She had nothing but fond memories of you at home.

To Don Peters, she would always want to thank you for giving her the opportunity to serve the union and its members. You gave her the opportunity, and God, did she serve. She served so well that she was to become the finest business agent in the entire International Brotherhood of Teamsters in just a very short time. Don, bringing her into the labor movement was the best decision that you have ever made.

To her stewards—how Regina treasured each of you. She loved working with you and helping you. Regina appreciated your kindness to her and the many wonderful things that you said about her. And certainly all the support that you gave her. She was especially excited when you had a party to honor her. It was certainly a wonderful night for her. She was truly thrilled by the marvelous comments about her.

On behalf of Don and myself, I want to express my gratitude to the stewards for inviting us to celebrate with her that night. It was a wonderful experience to attend and to be able to speak about Regina. I will share with you a secret that she shared with me. To the stewards of local 743, she always envied you. She always wanted to be a steward, working in a plant or an office or a warehouse, and never had that opportunity. At our Stewards' conference on May 9, 1981, a date that we mentioned earlier, Regina Polk made a speech to our stewards at that conference which was, in the opinion of all of those here, the finest speech ever given about the labor movement or any subject, for that matter. It was brilliant. She had the stewards on their feet on several occasions and the place, the hall, was on fire with excitement. Regina was a brilliant, brilliant speaker.

To the members of Local 743, you who were represented by Regina Polk. You know that you had the finest union representative, ever. She loved you and would do anything for you. Yes, her personal safety, her freedom, and even her life were yours. There was never a more dedicated person in the American labor movement.

To the unemployed workers, you lost a champion of your cause. She sympathized with you, she worked for you, and she certainly helped you.

To the office ladies of Local 743, Regina had a particular fondness for you. She was always interested in your welfare, and I can assure you that one of the real highlights of her Christmas season would be to go shopping to buy individual Christmas gifts for each of you. She certainly enjoyed each of you very much.

As Regina's closest friend, I would know what her message would be to you today. I'll share her thoughts with you now:

I believe that she would tell us to be good to one another.

She would tell us not to wait for a person to die or go on pension to say good things about them.

Regina would want us to speak up and never to hold back. She would want us to compliment each other and be kind to each other. She would tell us to say good things and not to wait. Don't wait to say "good job" or "thank you" or "I love you."

She was truly a magnificent woman.

In closing, let me share a little story with you. Regina would speak about this from time to time and it was her fantasy. The last time she spoke about this was two or three months ago. Regina would say, "I fantasize about this, Raymond. Someday, many years from now, when I'm an old lady, and maybe I'll have a cane, like my mom, you and I will be going into some fine restaurant downtown. I'll be wearing a new dress and an enormous hat. As we walk by two people at a table, we'll overhear one say to the other, "Who is that old broad?" and the other would say, "That's Regina Polk—she's a Teamster and one of the greatest women in the American labor movement."

Last Tuesday night, as Regina entered heaven after only 33 short years on Earth—the same number, by the way, that God gave to his son Jesus Christ—I'm sure someone would say, "Who was that magnificently beautiful young woman?" and the other person would reply, "That's Regina Polk. She's a Teamster. She was one of the greatest women ever in the American labor movement."

Twenty some years later people cry when they think about her, feeling the pain of loss while insisting that they had been blessed to have had her no matter how short the time. People she made feel special. People who want to meet her in heaven.

After the funeral, everyone realized the same thing: Nothing would return to normal. Nothing would ever be the same again. After packing up baby clothes earlier in the year, Johnnie Scott never dreamed that she would now be packing up Regina's clothing and giving it to as many people as she could find, to spare Tom more pain.

It took her a little longer to remove Regina's last note on the refrigerator to Tom: "I love you."

♥ Wrongful Death

*I*n 1985 Eugene Pavalon of Pavalon, Gifford & Laatsch represented the estate of Regina Polk in a wrongful death suit cast against Air Illinois.

Don Peters testified at the trial that he expected Regina to be president of the Teamsters Local 743 at some point in time. The woman who was once considered a threat to male supremacy in the Teamsters had by then developed a loyal following among members and management, politicians, and thugs.

In an odd twist of fate, one of the jurors, a woman by the name of Lois McKee, was listening to the testimony being given when suddenly she realized, "*I am wearing her clothes! This is the same person that Johnnie was talking about!* It was just too coincidental."

"I didn't know until she came back from jury duty because she couldn't talk about it," remembers Johnnie. "Afterwards, she told me, 'I was sitting there and realized, *My God, I've got on the woman's clothes!*'"

The jury returned a verdict in the amount of $1.5 million, which at the time was the second-highest monetary award ever for the wrongful death of a female in the state of Illinois. The verdict was affirmed by the Illinois Appellate Court on appeal.

Regina V. Polk Memorial Fund Board, 1984, from left, standing: Thomas Heagy; Edna Hunter, steward at the University of Chicago; Ray Kujawa, steward at Chicago State University; Dorla Wuertemburg, steward at the University of Chicago; and Ray Hamilton, Local 743 trustee. Seated: Phyllis Bacon, steward at Governors State University; Mollie Galloway and Maggie Newman, stewards at the University of Chicago.

Regina V. Polk Memorial Fund Benefit, March 1985, center: Eileen Cordova (Regina's sister), Johnnie Scott (to the right), and Tom Heagy.

142

The Regina V. Polk Scholarship Fund for Labor Leadership

Shortly after Regina died, a group of union stewards at the University of Chicago met in Maggie Newman's office to hold yet another in a continuing series of wakes. Grieving, smoking, and crying, they decided finally to do something to remember Regina by and came upon the idea to create scholarships to train women for leadership roles in labor.

"To organize women," says Newman, "you need people like Regina for people to admire and look up to and say, 'Wow, that's so great.' The labor movement needs to find and nurture them. We need scholarships to help guide them into leadership roles."

They approached Regina's widower, Tom Heagy, who made a substantial contribution of money from the court settlement, making it basically an endowed fund. Later, there were bake sales and days at the races, which were attended by owners of the companies she had unionized. "They gave," says Phyllis Bacon, "because they wanted to do something to resolve their grief."

The Regina V. Polk Scholarship Fund for Labor Leadership was created. The original trustees were Tom Heagy, Ray Hamilton, Sarah

Brown, Joel D'Alba, and Melva Hunter. The original stewards' committee members were Phyllis Bacon, Paula Degnan, Mollie Galloway, Edna Hunter, Ray Kujawa, Maggie Newman, and Dorla Wuertemburg.

Regina believed that the future of the labor movement depends on developing creative leadership. To that end, the Regina V. Polk Scholarship Fund for Labor Leadership has underwritten programs such as the following:

University of Illinois' Regina V. Polk Women's Leadership Conference

This three-day conference brings together active union women from Illinois and beyond in an informal learning environment. The conference focuses on collective bargaining, with workshops, lectures, and discussion groups that contribute to organizing, networking, leadership skills, and effectiveness at the negotiating table.

DePaul University's Regina Polk High School Program

This program teaches high school students about unions and collective bargaining. More than 2,000 students in the Chicago metropolitan area, Peoria, and Champaign have participated. The three-day program consists of visiting the high schools and talking to the students about Regina Polk and unions and explaining collective bargaining (at some sites by role-play). The students also learn about labor history by taking a tour of the Pullman historic district.

University of Illinois' Midwest School for Women Workers Summer Seminar for Labor Leadership and Law

On the recommendation of their unions, women participate in

this five-day program, which consists of general labor education with an emphasis on labor history. Through its varied courses, union women are taught about union leadership, arbitration, international labor, and labor law.

Teamsters Local 743 President's Scholarship

The annual scholarships awarded through this program are to the dependent children or stepchildren of Local 743 members to help further their education. The recipients must be current high school graduating seniors or previous 743 scholarship winners, who can apply for additional scholarships to assist them in their second, third, and fourth years of college.

Since the Regina V. Polk Foundation was founded in 1983, it has made $780,000 in grants benefiting more than 650 women—not counting the students in the high school program. Through the foundation, Regina's spirit is alive—teaching new generations of women how to fight for their rights and all employees' rights.

Every year the fund has a reception at which union people come to tell their stories about working with Regina, being touched by Regina, being organized because of Regina. People whose lives, whose families' lives, were improved because of her life.

Which of the women funded by the Polk Foundation will have the same combination of intelligence, compassion, and drive to go out now when the stakes are so high, the leaders so diminished, and the opposition so great? Who will be able to emerge from Regina V. Polk's shadow, put on her makeup, and fight the kind of fights that are needed today? Fights that Regina might have won *if she had lived.*

This is not the end but actually the beginning. Regina Polk did all she could to redress human wrongs. Now it's our turn. To care. And it's a big job.

"When the gates of heaven swung open that night," says Melva Hunter,"
and someone asked, 'Who is that beautiful young woman?' I hope they said,
'Her? She's a Teamster.'"

♥ Epilogue

███████████████████████████

I was in bed. Gina was with me and she brought two little kittens and cut off the end of the ear of one of them and I said, "Gina, we aren't keeping these kittens," but she didn't say anything, and then I noticed that Morgan was on my lap like he used to be and I said, "Gina, Morgan's back."

And then I realized it wasn't Gina but only an apparition and although I could barely hear it before she disappeared, she said, "I love you," and I said, "I love you."

And then I awoke.

And I felt I had been visited by her spirit.

—Tom Heagy, November 20, 1983

Index

A

Air Illinois, 133
    crash of, 134
    wrongful death suit against, 141
air traffic controllers, 103, 129
Aldens, 124, 125, 126, 128
Alexander, Albert, 112
American Federation of State, County, and Municipal Employees, 58
anti-unionism, 106, 107, 108, 130

B

Bacon, Phyllis, 90, 91, 92, 93, 125, 143, 144
Beck, Dave, 101
Blue Cross/Blue Shield, 40, 50, 57, 58, 61
Booth, Paul, 58, 131
Brown, Sarah, 1, 45, 81, 82, 83, 95, 143–144
Burack, Amy, 78, 80
Butler Brothers, 37

C

Cannon, Howard W., 130
Carroll, Muriel, 40, 58
Carter, Shelley, 16, 17, 18, 19, 20, 22, 25, 26, 27, 80, 95
Chicago Maroon, 122, 123
Chicago State University, 87, 88, 89, 90, 91
Civil Air Patrol, 12
Civil Rights Act, 112

Simpson, Bob, 33, 35, 37, 39, 50, 52, 54, 55, 56, 60, 64, 68, 70, 72,
73, 81, 82, 118
criticism of, 131
description of, 53
Regina Polk, clash with, 61
Smith, Jonathan Z., 121, 122, 123
South Shore Bank, 44
Spiegel's, 124
State University Merit Classification System, 89
St. Joseph's Hospital, 117
Swedenborg, Emanuel, 77

T

Teamsters. *See* International Brotherhood of Teamsters
Teamsters Local 743, 33, 35, 37, 38, 39, 51, 66, 68, 104, 111, 127,
136, 138, 141.
See also International Brotherhood of Teamsters
atmosphere at, 50
as male dominated, 39, 50, 58
and President's Scholarship, 145
racism at, 50, 54–56, 104, 141
sexism at, 56, 58
tension at, 53–54
Thompson, James R., 128, 133
Travolta, John, 91

U

United Brotherhood of Teamsters Central States Pension Fund, 55,
101, 103
University of California at Berkeley, 22
University of Chicago, 28, 87, 91, 92, 93, 115.
See also University of Chicago Hospital

Publisher's Credits
Cover design by Timothy Kocher. Interior design and layout by Mike Wykowski. Scans by Mike Wykowski. Editing by Laura R. Gabler. Proofreading by Sharon Woodhouse. Index by June Sawyer.

Acknowledgments

$\mathcal{T}$his book is dedicated to the late Tom Hamilton, son of Ray Hamilton, and the late Johnnie Scott. The texture and nuance of Regina's life at Local 743 and at home with Tom Heagy would not have been possible if it weren't for their insights and colorful narratives.

I would like to thank my predecessor on this book, Bob Breving, whose interviews with many of the subjects and knowledge of labor provided a foundation as well as a running start into the fascinating life of Regina Polk.

I would also like to thank every single person who shared their memories of Regina with Bob and me—most importantly, her husband, Tom Heagy, and sister, Eileen Cordova, but also Paul Boothe, Shelley Carter, Robert Simpson Jr., Don Peters, Amy Burack, Mike Burack, Ted Marmor, Ray Hamilton, Joel D'Alba, Vicki Saporta, Maggie Newman, Sarah Brown, Edna Hunter, Phyllis Bacon, Ray Kujawa, Gary Mamlin, Melva Hunter, Robert McAllister, Paul Booth, Sirlena Perry, and Lois McKee. Thanks also to Pat Lofthouse for her research.

Finally, I would like to thank Regina's husband, Tom Heagy, for giving me the opportunity to explore the life of one of the most fascinating American women I have ever had the privilege to come to know.

About the Author

*J*erry **Spencer Hesser** has had the pleasure of telling stories in print, on television, and on the stage for three decades. A recipient of the Corporation for Public Broadcasting Gold Award, three Emmys, and a host of other honors, she has searched for vampires in Transylvania, Limburger Cheese in Wisconsin, the meaning of a black canvas at The Art Institute of Chicago, and told the life stories of people ranging from Robert McCormick to Regina Polk. She has also taught children about AIDS and adults about mental illness. Her book *Kissing Doorknobs* received an ALA award and her play about Elvis was called "the funniest show in town" by FOX News. She has enjoyed working with Audrey Hepburn, Oprah Winfrey, and R. Kelly. Her story on Mackinac Island documents one perfect summer day on Michigan's treasured island. Terry is currently working on two more programs on islands without cars (Sark, in the English Channel; and Hydra, in Greece) and is busy documenting Homer Bryant's Chicago Multi-Cultural Dance Center. An avid skier, former scuba diver, and boxing fan, Terry is a world traveler and eager student of…whatever captures her imagination next.

Lake Claremont Press

Founded in 1994, Lake Claremont Press specializes in books on the Chicago area and its history, focusing on preserving the city's past, exploring its present environment, and cultivating a strong sense of place for the future. Visit us on the Web at www.lakeclaremont.com.

Selected Booklist

Rule 53: Capturing Hippies, Spies, Politicians and Murderers in an American Courtroom

Today's Chicago Blues

A Chicago Tavern: A Goat, a Curse, and the American Dream

Wrigley Field's Last World Series: The Wartime Chicago Cubs and the Pennant of 1945

On the Job: Behind the Stars of the Chicago Police Department

Graveyards of Chicago: The People, History, Art, and Lore of Cook County Cemeteries

Great Chicago Fires: Historic Blazes That Shaped a City

Chicago TV Horror Movie Shows: From Shock Theatre to Svengoolie

The Golden Age of Chicago Children's Television

From Lumber Hookers to the Hooligan Fleet: A Treasury of Chicago Maritime History

The Chicago River: A Natural and Unnatural History

The Politics of Place: A History of Zoning in Chicago

Near West Side Stories: Struggles for Community in Chicago's Maxwell Street Neighborhood

For Members Only: A History and Guide to Chicago's Oldest Private Clubs